EASY PIANO

POPULAR SHEET MUSIC HITS

Arranged by DAN COATES

Published 2004

Griffin House 161 Hammersmith Road London W6 8BS England

Editorial management: Artemis Music Limited (www.artemismusic.com)

Amazed

Words and Music by Marv Green, Aimee Mayo and Chris Lindsey

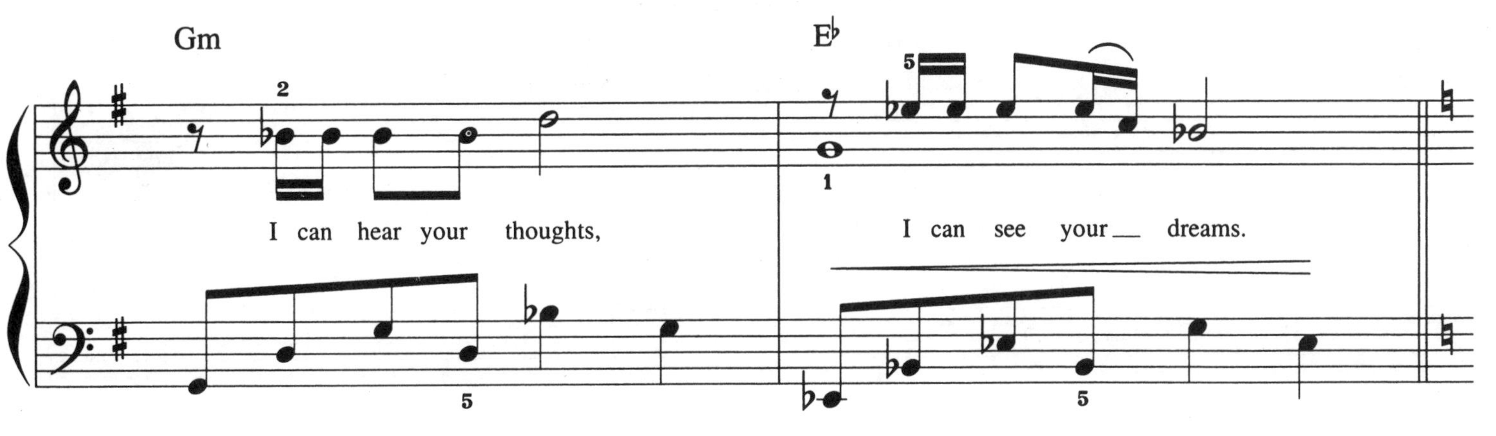
Gm
E♭
I can hear your thoughts,
I can see your dreams.

Chorus:
C
G
I don't know how you do what you do.
I'm so in love with
mf

Am
F
you.
It just keeps get - ting bet - ter.

C
G
I wan - na spend the rest of my life
with you by my side

Am
G
F
for - ev - er and ev - er.
E♭
F
Ev - 'ry lit - tle thing that you do, ba - by, I'm a - mazed by
1.
G
D
you.
dim.
2.
G
B♭
C
you.
mf

G
B♭
F
C
G
Ev - 'ry lit - tle thing that you do,
I'm so in love with
Am
F
you. It just keeps get - ting bet - ter.
C
G
I wan - na spend the rest of my life
with you by my side

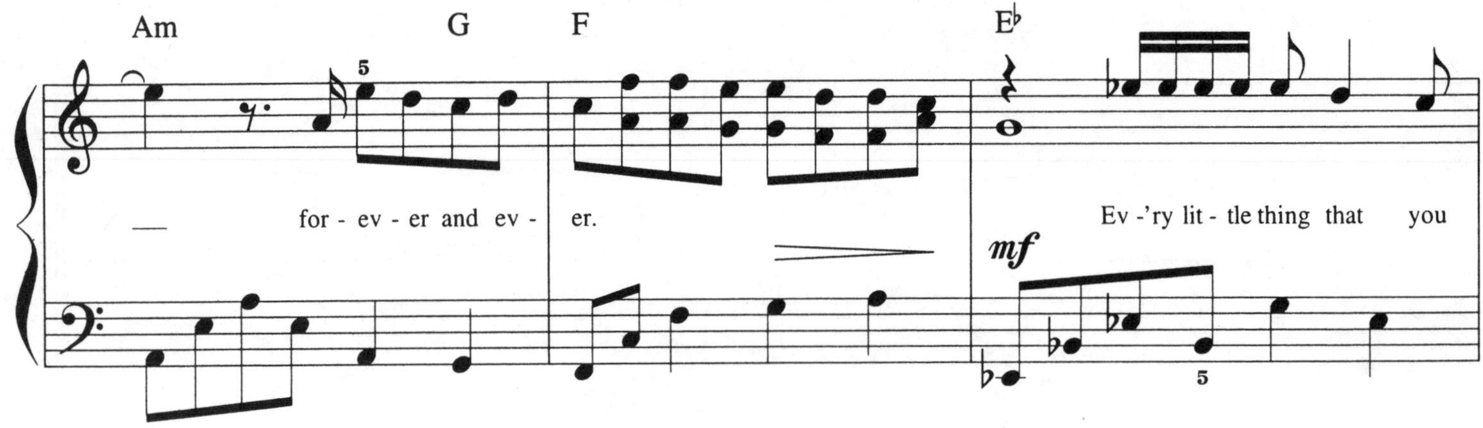

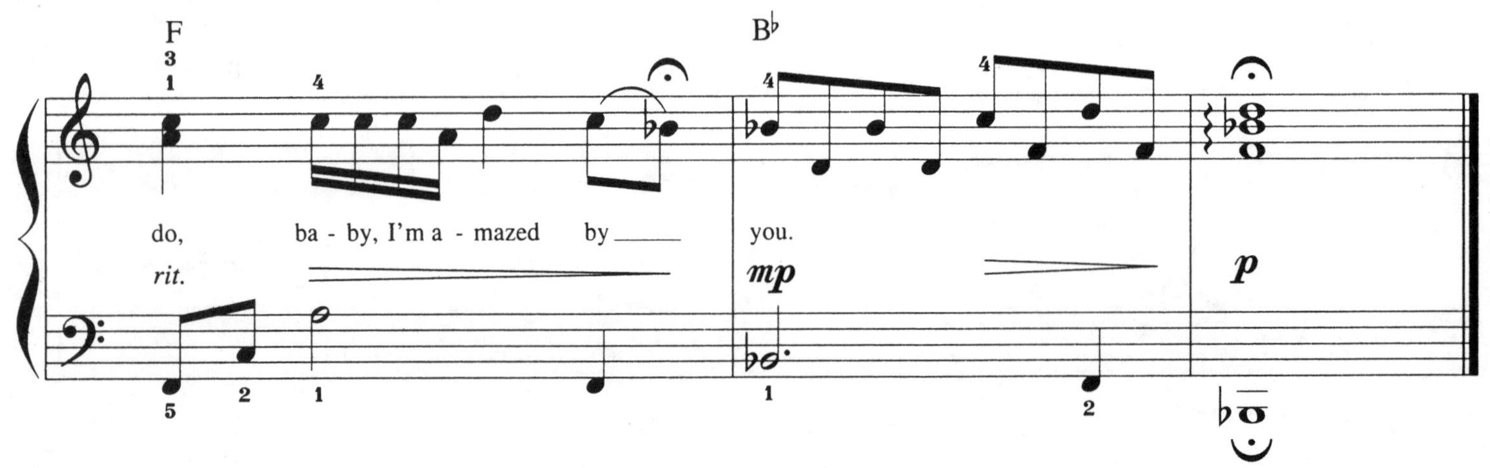

Verse 2:
The smell of your skin,
The taste of your kiss,
The way you whisper in the dark.
Your hair all around me,
Baby, you surround me.
You touch every place in my heart.
Oh, it feels like the first time every time.
I wanna spend the whole night in your eyes.
(To Chorus:)

As Time Goes By

Words and Music by Herman Hupfeld

C
A7
Dm7
G7
And when two lov - ers woo, they
Gm
G7
C
Dm7
still say, "I love you," on that you can re - ly;
D♯dim7
C/E
Am7
D7
no mat - ter what the fu - ture
Dm7
G7
C
F
Fm
C
C7
brings, as time goes by.
F
A7
Moon - light and love songs nev - er out of date,
mf

Dm D#dim Am F7
hearts full of pas-sion, jeal-ous-y and hate; wo-man needs man and
D7 G7 C#dim7 Dm7 G7
man must have his mate; that no one can de - ny. It's
Dm7 G7 Gm G7
still the same old sto - ry, a fight for love and glo - ry, a
mp
C Dm7 D#dim7 C/E Am7 D7
case of do or die! The world will al - ways wel - come
(cresc.)
mf
C A7 Dm7 G G+ 1. C A7 2. C
lov - ers, as time goes by. You by.
mp
p

Can't Fight The Moonlight

Words and Music by Diane Warren

Moderate, steady beat (♩= 98)

Verse:
Bm
Em
A
1. Un-der a lov - er's sky, gon-na be with you, and no
2. There's no es - cape from love. Once the gen - tle breeze weaves
mf

G
Bm
Em
one's gon-na be a-round. If you think that you won't fall, we'll just wait
it's spell up-on your heart, no mat-ter what you think, it won't be

A
Em
until, 'til the sun goes down. Un-der-neath the star-
too long 'til you're in my arms. Un-der-neath the star-

D
Em
D/F♯
light, star - light, there's a mag - i - cal feel - ing so right.
light, star - light, we'll be lost in a rhy - thm so right.

Chorus:
G
It will take you in to-night.
Feel it steal your heart to-night.
You can try to re-sist, try to hide
Cm
f
Fm
B♭
A♭
G
from my kiss, but you know, but you know that you can't fight the moon-light. Deep
Cm
Fm
B♭
in the dark, you'll sur-ren-der your heart. Don't you know, don't you know that you
1.
A♭
G7
Fm
G7
can't fight the moon-light, no, you can't fight it. It's
G/B
2.
Fm
G7
gon-na get to your heart.
no, you can't fight it.

Fm7
G7
No mat-ter what you do, the night is gon-na get to you.
Bridge:
Bm7
Em7
A
mf
Can't fight it. Don't try it, you're
Em
D
nev-er gon-na win, 'cause un-der-neath the star-light, star-light,
Em
D/F♯
there's a mag-i-cal feel-ing so right.
G
It will steal your heart to-night. You can try

Chorus:

Cm
Fm
B♭
to re - sist, try to hide from my kiss, but you know, but you know that you
f

A♭
G7
Cm
Fm
can't fight the moon - light. Deep in the dark, you'll sur - ren - der your heart. Don't you know,

B♭
A♭
G7
Fm
don't you know that you can't fight the moon - light, no, you can't fight

1.
2.
G7
G7
it. You can try it. It's gon-na get to your heart.
mp

Foolish Games

Words and Music by Jewel Kilcher

Dm
B♭
3
And I watched from my win - dow, al - ways felt I was
F
C
1.3.
2.4.
out - side look - ing in on you.
Bridge:
Gm
B♭
In case you failed to no - tice, in case you failed to see,
mf
F
C
this is my heart bleed - ing be - fore you, this is me down on my knees.

Chorus:
B♭
C
These fool - ish games are
f
F
C/E
Dm
tear - ing me a - part, and
B♭
C
your thought - less words are
F
C/E
B♭
break - ing my heart. You're break - ing my
dim.
mp
3

Verse 2:
You're always the mysterious one
With dark eyes and careless hair,
You were fashionably sensitive
But too cool to care.
You stood in my doorway with nothing to say
Besides some comment on the weather.
(To Bridge:)

Verse 3:
You're always brilliant in the morning,
Smoking your cigarettes and talking over coffee.
Your philosophies on art, Baroque moved you.
You loved Mozart and you'd speak of your loved ones
As I clumsily strummed my guitar.

Verse 4:
You'd teach me of honest things,
Things that were daring, things that were clean.
Things that knew what an honest dollar did mean.
I hid my soiled hands behind my back.
Somewhere along the line,
I must have gone off track with you.

Bridge 2:
Excuse me, I think I've mistaken you
For somebody else,
Somebody who gave a damn,
Somebody more like myself.
(To Chorus:)

Genie In A Bottle

Words and Music by Pamela Sheyne, David Frank and Steve Kipner

Gm F E♭
licking your lips and blowing kisses my way, but that don't mean I'm gonna give it away,
Hormones racing at the speed of light, but that don't mean it's got to be tonight,
Gm F E♭ Gm F
baby, baby, baby.
baby, baby, baby.
Oh
E♭ Dm7 Gm F E♭ Dm7
oh.
Gm F E♭ Dm Gm F
f
If you want to be with me, baby, there's a price to pay. I'm a genie in a
E♭ D7 Gm F
bottle, you gotta rub me the right way. If you want to be with

E♭ Dm Gm F
me, I can make your wish come true. You got - ta make a big im -
E♭ D7 To Coda ⊕ Gm F
pres - sion, I got - ta like what you do. I'm a ge - nie in a bot - tle, ba - by,
mf
E♭ Dm7 Gm F
you got - ta rub __ me the right way, hon - ey. I'm a ge - nie in a bot - tle, ba - by,
1. 2.
E♭maj7 E♭maj7
come, come, come on and let me out. come, come, come on and let me out.
Gm F E♭ Dm7
I'm a ge - nie in a bot - tle, ba - by, you got - ta rub __ me the right way, hon - ey.

D.S. al Coda
Gm
F
E♭maj7
I'm a ge - nie in a bot - tle, ba - by,
come, come, come on and let me out.
Coda
Gm
F
E♭
Dm
Gm
F
f
If you want to be with
me, ba - by, there's a price to
pay. I'm a ge - nie in a
E♭
D7
Gm
F
bot - tle, you got - ta rub me the right
way. If you want to be with
E♭
Dm
Gm
F
E♭
D7
me, I can make your wish come
true. Just come and set me
free, ba - by, and I'll be with you.
Gm
(No Chord)
I'm a ge - nie in a bot - tle, ba - by,
mp
come, come, come on and let me out.

The Greatest Love Of All

Words by Linda Creed
Music by Michael Masser

C
C+
C6
C7
be. Ev-'ry-bod-y's search-ing for a he -ro,
peo-ple need some-one to look up___ to,
F
F+
F6
F+
I nev-er found an-y - one who ful - filled___ that
need; a lone - ly
Em
Am
Dm
F/G
G
place to be, so I
learned to de - pend on
F
C/E
Dm7
Dm7/G
me. I de - cid - ed long___ a - go
nev-er to walk in an-y - one's shad-ow;
F
C/E
Dm7
Dm7/G
if I fail,___ if I suc-ceed,___ at
least I lived___ as I be-lieve, and no

F C/E Dm7 Dm7/G
mat-ter what — they take from me, they can't take a - way my dig - ni - ty;
Em Am Dm G7
Be-cause the great - est love of all is hap-pen - ing to
Em Am Dm G7 Em Am
me. I found the great - est
Dm F/G G C C7 Am Dm7
love of all in-side of me. The great-est love of all
Gm7 C7 Am Dm Gm7 C7
is eas - y to a - chieve, learn-ing to

Am Dm Gm C7
1.
F G
love your-self is the great - est love of all.
Em Am Dm F/G G
2.
F
mp
all. And
G7 Em Am Dm G7
if by chance that spe - cial place that you've been dream-ing
Em Am Dm G7 Em Am
of leads you to a lone - ly place,
Dm F C/E Dm7 G7 C
find your strength in love.
pp

How Do I Live

Words and Music by Diane Warren

C
Bm7
Em7
world, my heart, my soul. If
you ev - er leave,
cresc.
Am7
Bm7
Em7
B♭/C
C7
ba - by, you would take a - way ev - 'ry - thing
good in my life.
And tell me
F
C
B♭
C7
F
C
now, how do I live with - out
you? I want to know.
How do I breathe with - out
mf
B♭
Am7
Dm
Gm7
Am7
B♭
you, if you ev - er go?
How do I ev - er,
ev - er sur - vive?

To Coda
1.
Gm7/C
F
C/D
How do I,
how do I,
oh, how do I
live?
2. With - out you
mp
2.
Gm7/C
F
Am7
Gm7
how do I,
oh, how do I
live?
mp
Dm7
Am7
D7sus4
D7
cresc.
If
Bm7
Em7
Am7
you ev - er leave,
ba - by, you would take a - way ev - 'ry - thing.
mf

Verse 2:
Without you, there'd be no sun in my sky,
There would be no love in my life,
There'd be no world left for me.
And I, baby, I don't know what I would do,
I'd be lost if I lost you.
If you ever leave,
Baby, you would take away everything
Real in my life.
And tell me now...
(To Chorus:)

I Could Not Ask For More

Words and Music by Diane Warren

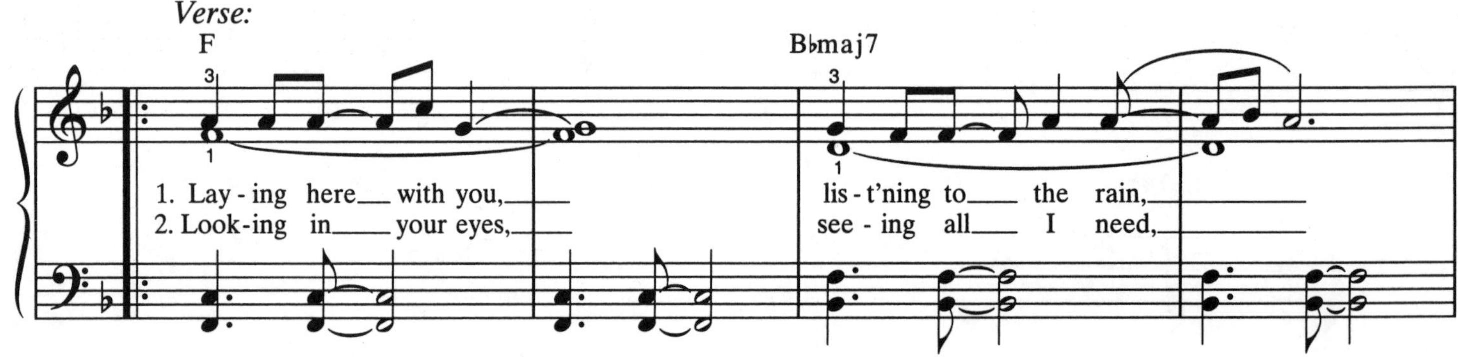

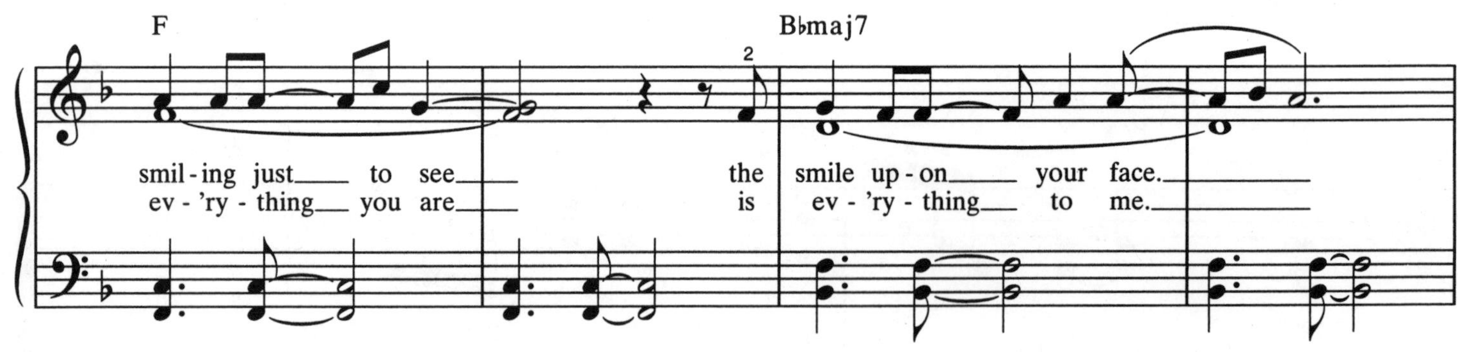

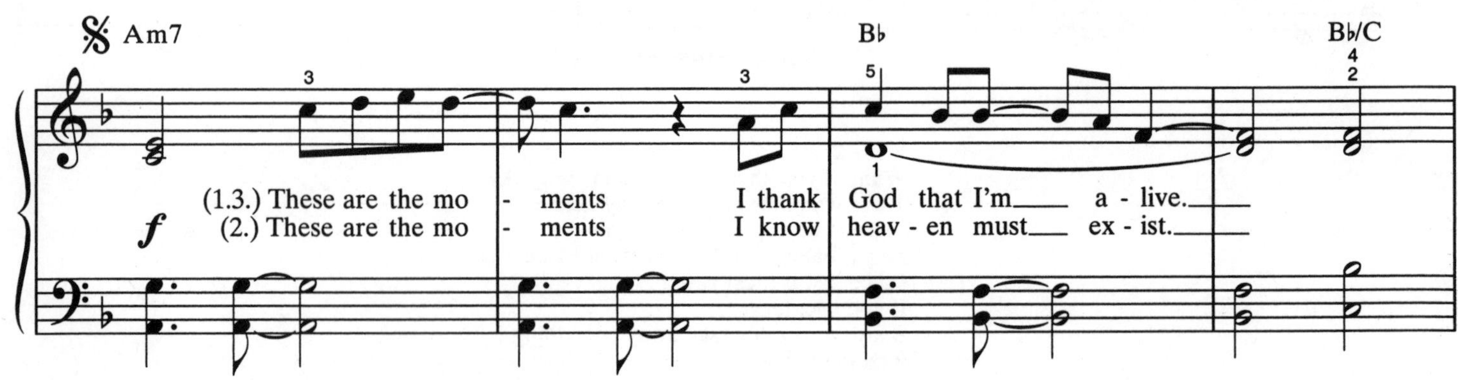

Am7
Dm7
G7
These are the mo - ments I'll re - mem - ber all my life. I found
These are the mo - ments I know all I need is this. I have

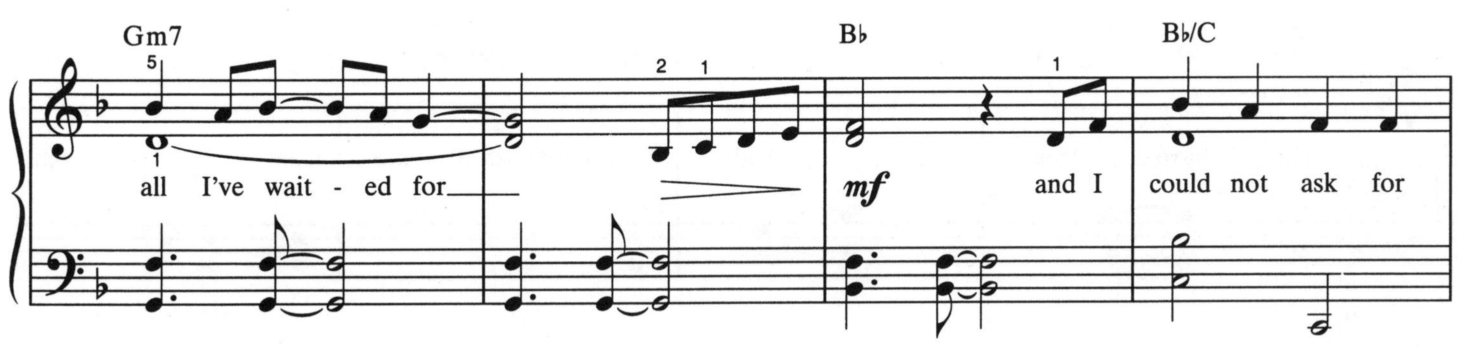
Gm7
B♭
B♭/C
all I've wait - ed for
mf
and I could not ask for

1.
F
B♭maj7
2.3.
F
more.
more.

Chorus:
B♭
I could not ask for more than this time to - geth - er. I could not ask for
f

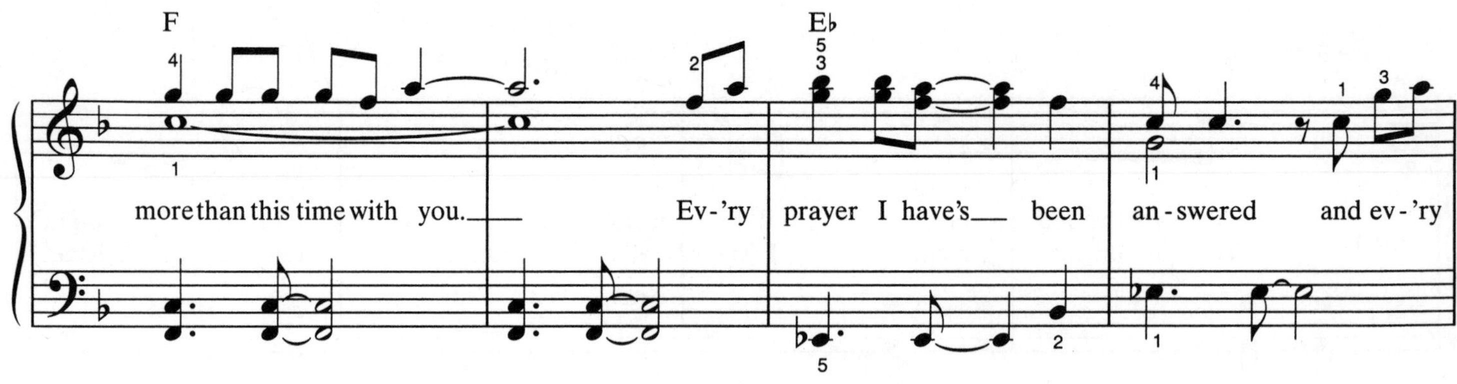
F
E♭
more than this time with you.
Ev-'ry
prayer I have's been
an-swered and ev-'ry

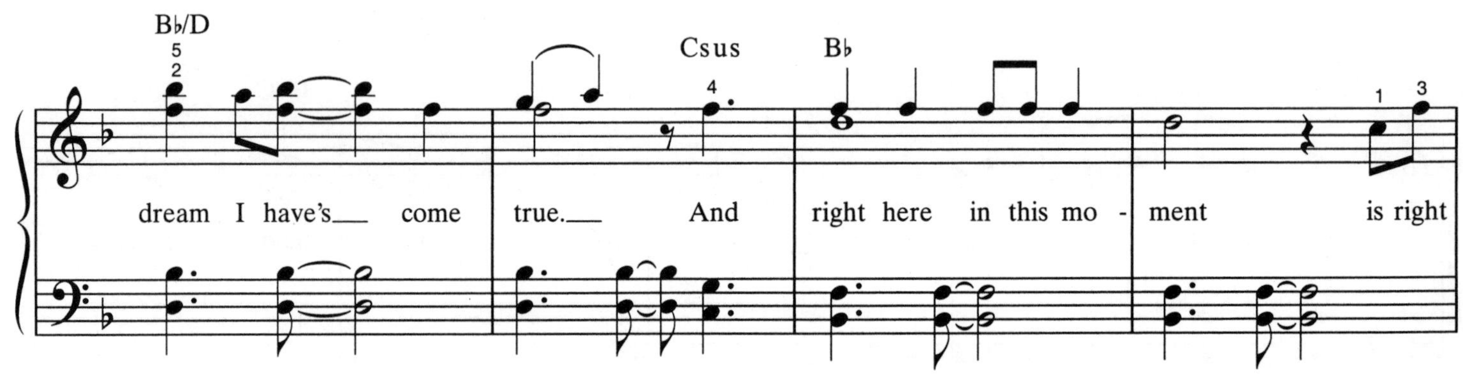
B♭/D
Csus
B♭
dream I have's come
true. And
right here in this mo-
ment is right

To Coda
F
Fm/A♭
Fm
where I'm meant to be.
Oh,
here with you,
here with

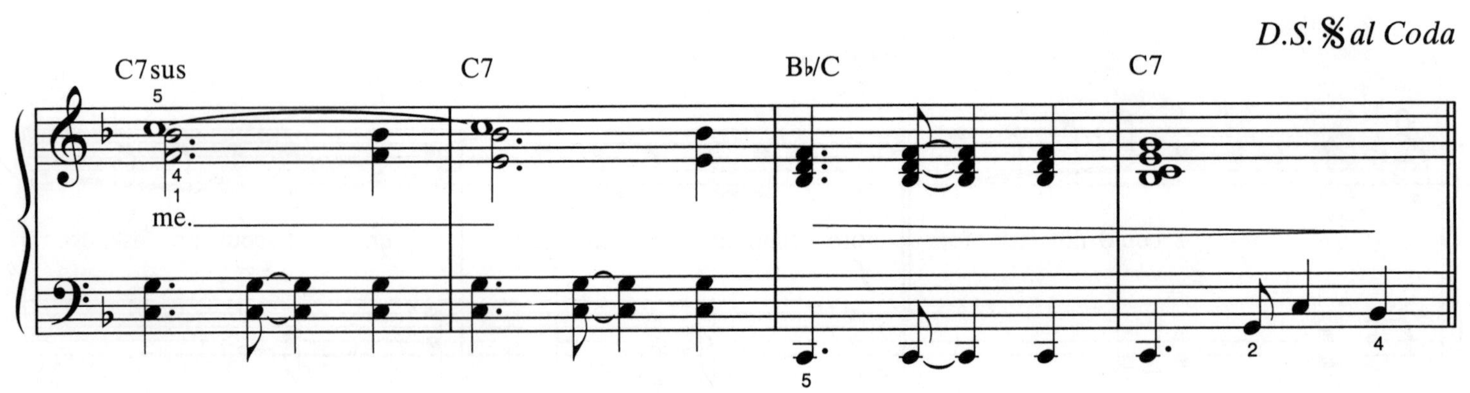
D.S. al Coda
C7sus
C7
B♭/C
C7
me.

Coda
C7sus
C7
B♭
me.
I could not ask for
more than the love you give
f

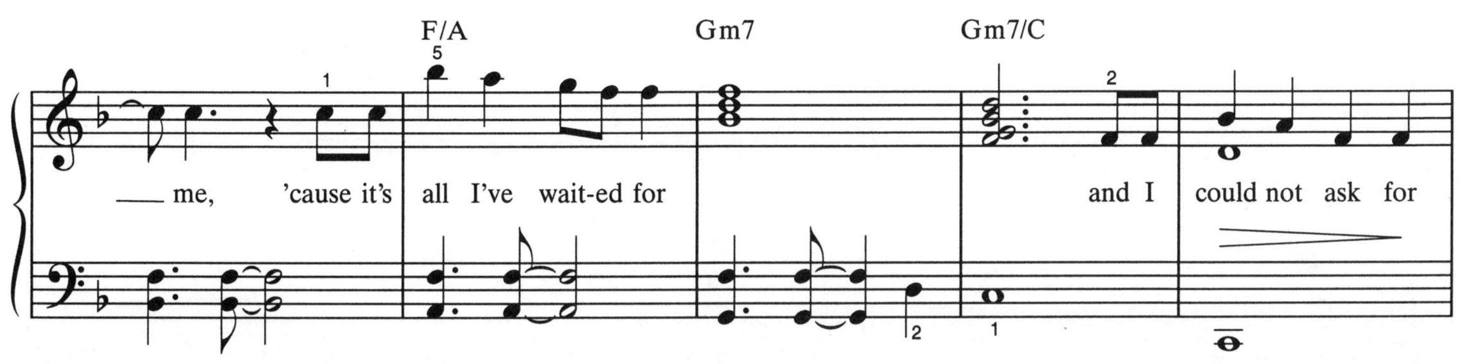
F/A
Gm7
Gm7/C
me, 'cause it's
all I've wait-ed for
and I
could not ask for

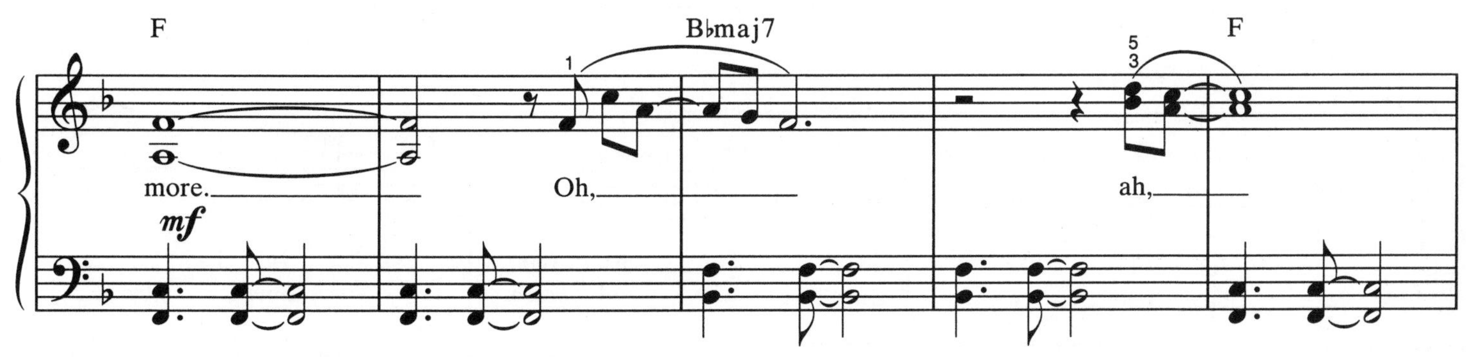
F
B♭maj7
F
more.
mf
Oh,
ah,

B♭maj7
B♭/C
F
oh
yeah.
And I
could not ask for
rit. e dim.
more.
mp

Because You Loved Me

Words and Music by Diane Warren

Gm7/C
E♭
Dm7
be for - ev - er thank - ful, ba - by.
grate - ful for each day you gave me.
You're the one who held
May - be I don't know
mf
Gm7
me up,
that much, but I
nev - er let me fall.
know this much is true:
B♭m7
B♭/C
You're the one who saw me through,
I was blessed be - cause I was
through it all.
loved by you.
F
You were my
strength when I was weak,
you were my
mp

B♭
Dm
voice when I could - n't speak.
You were my
eyes when I could - n't see,
you saw the
B♭/C
best there was in me.
cresc.
C7
Lift - ed me
Am7
up when I could - n't reach,
mf
you gave me
B♭
E♭maj7
faith 'cause you be - lieved.
I'm
Gm7/C
ev - 'ry - thing I am
be - cause you
To Coda

1.
F
B♭/C
loved me.
2. You gave me
mp
2.
F
A7
loved me.
You were al - ways there
mp
mf
Dm7
for me, the ten - der wind that car - ried me. A
A7
Dm
light in the dark,
shin - ing your love in - to my life.

Gm7
You've been my in - spi - ra - tion, through the
f
F/A
C7sus4
lies, you were the truth. My world is a bet - ter place
B♭/C
D.S. al Coda
because of you. You were my
Coda
F
Gm7/C
loved me. I'm ev - 'ry - thing I am
mp
F
be - cause you loved me.
p

I Turn To You

Words and Music by Diane Warren

mf legato

(with pedal)

mp

1. When I'm lost

Verse:

F | C/E | B♭/D | B♭/C | C7

— in the rain, — in your eyes I know I'll find the light to light my way. — When I'm scared, —

— the will to win, — I just reach for you and I can reach the sky a - gain. — I can do —

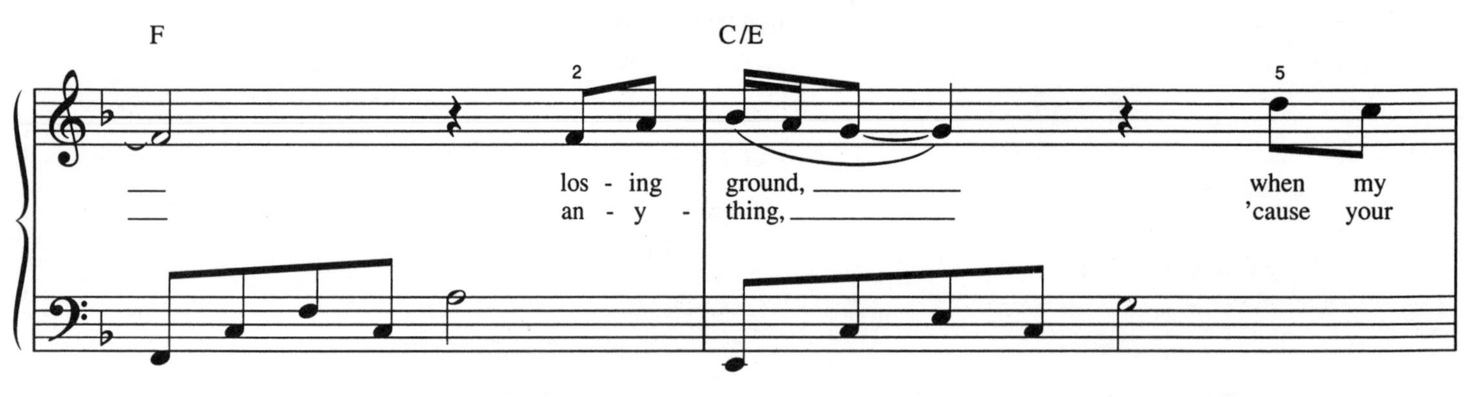
F
C/E
los - ing ground, when my
an - y - thing, 'cause your

A♭maj7
Gm7
world is go - ing cra - zy, you can turn it all a - round.
love is so a - maz - ing, 'cause your love in - spi - res me.

A7
Dm
And when I'm down, you're there, push - ing me to the top.
And when I need a friend, you're al - ways on my side,

Gm7
C7sus
You're al - ways there giv - ing me all you've got.
giv - ing me faith, tak - ing me through the night.
For a shield

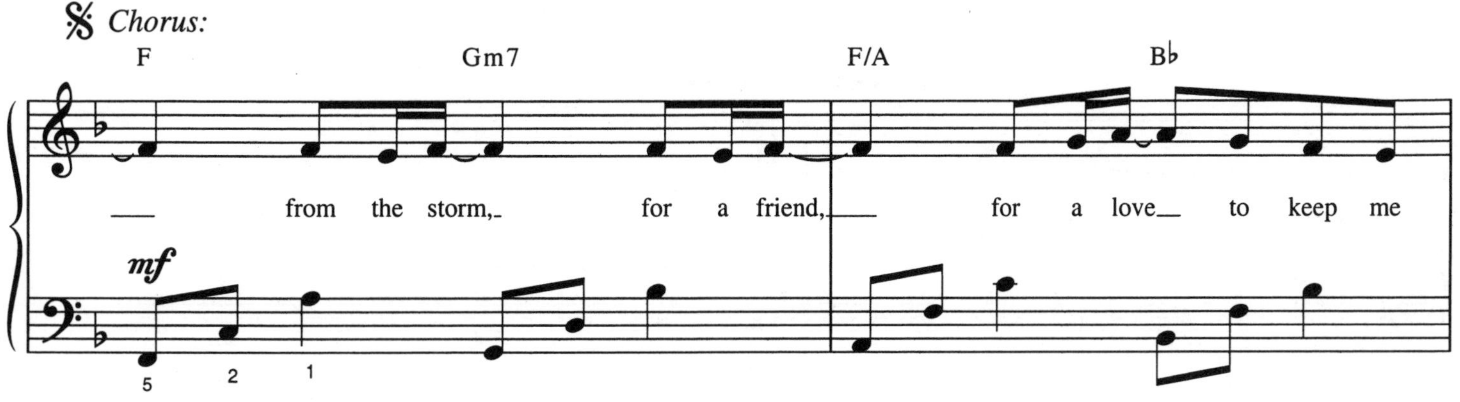

Chorus:
F
Gm7
F/A
B♭
mf
from the storm, for a friend, for a love to keep me

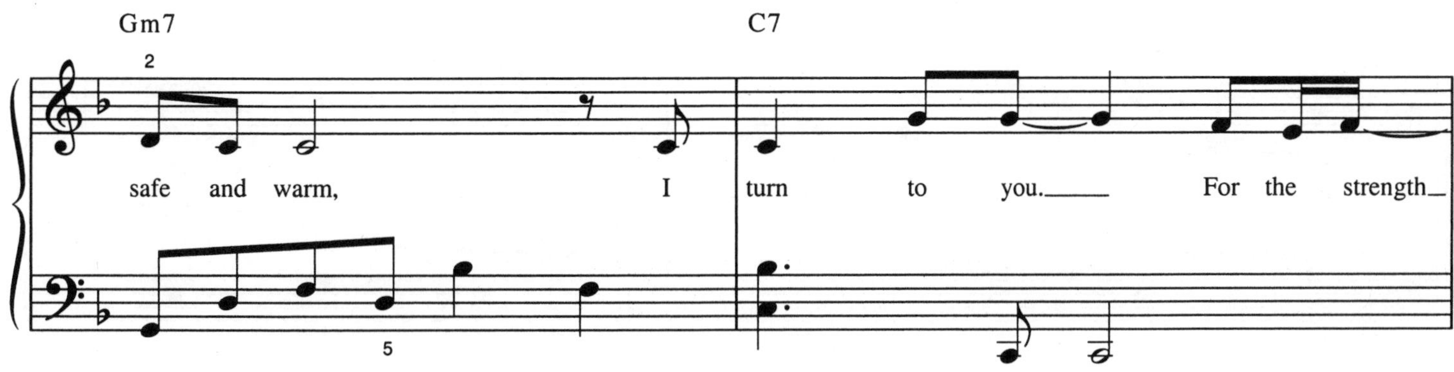

Gm7
C7
safe and warm, I turn to you. For the strength

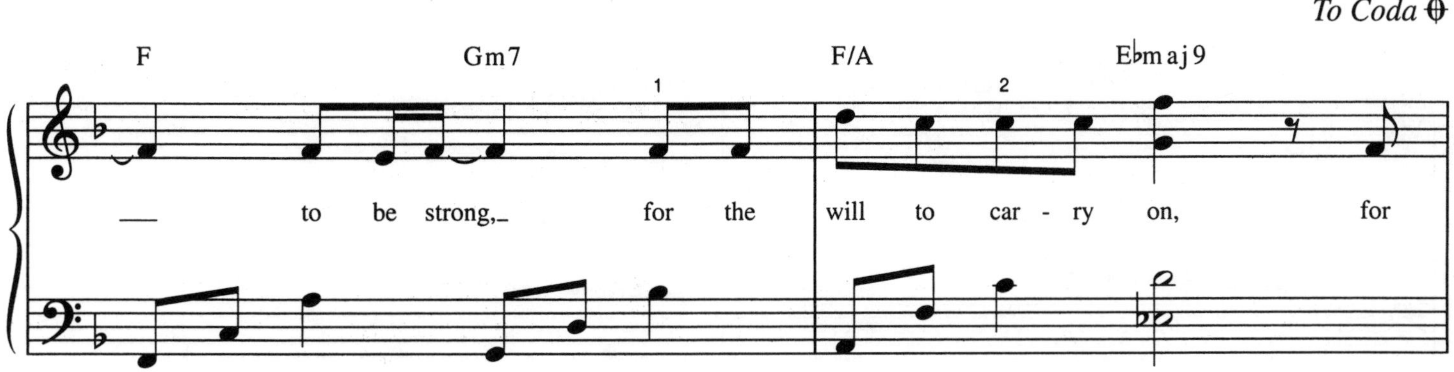

To Coda
F
Gm7
F/A
E♭maj9
to be strong, for the will to car - ry on, for

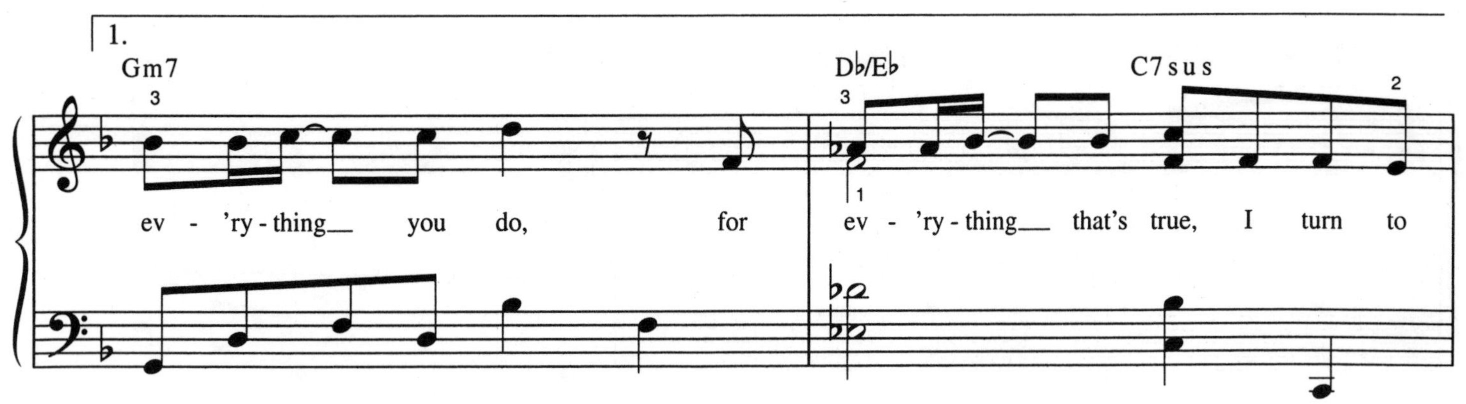

1.
Gm7
D♭/E♭
C7sus
ev - 'ry - thing you do, for ev - 'ry - thing that's true, I turn to

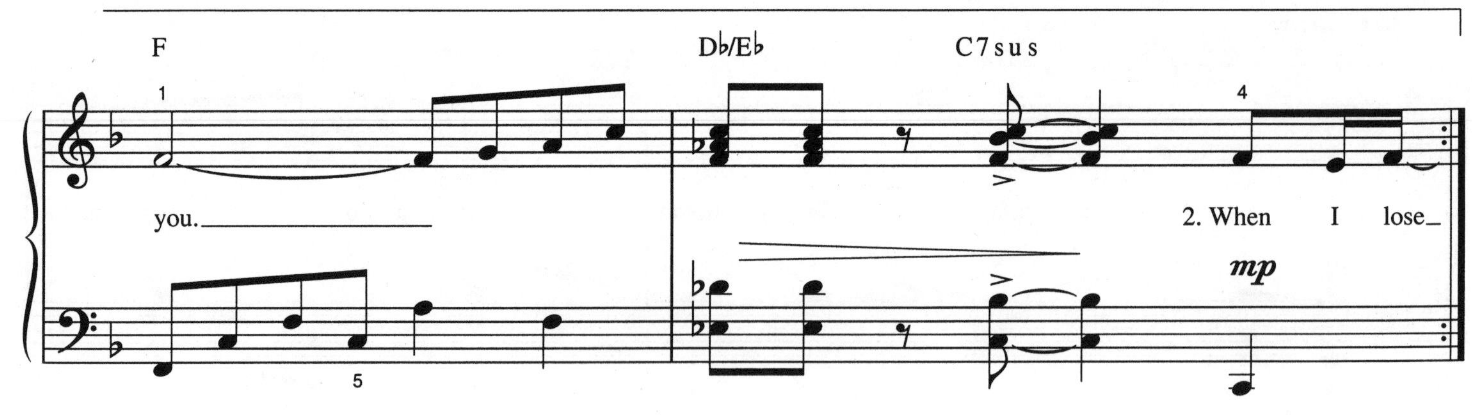
F
Db/Eb
C7sus
you.
2. When I lose
mp

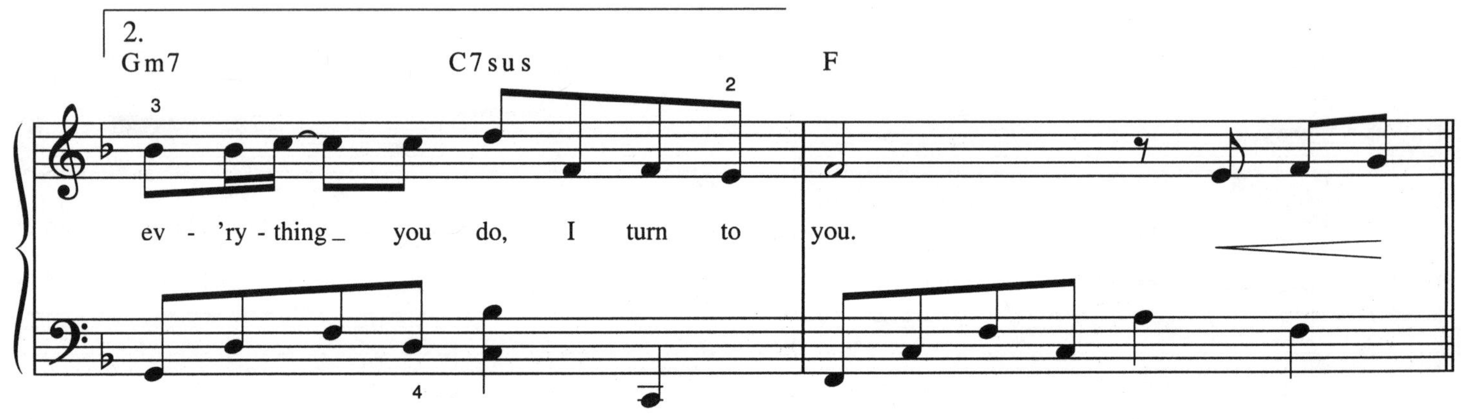
2.
Gm7
C7sus
F
ev - 'ry - thing you do, I turn to
you.

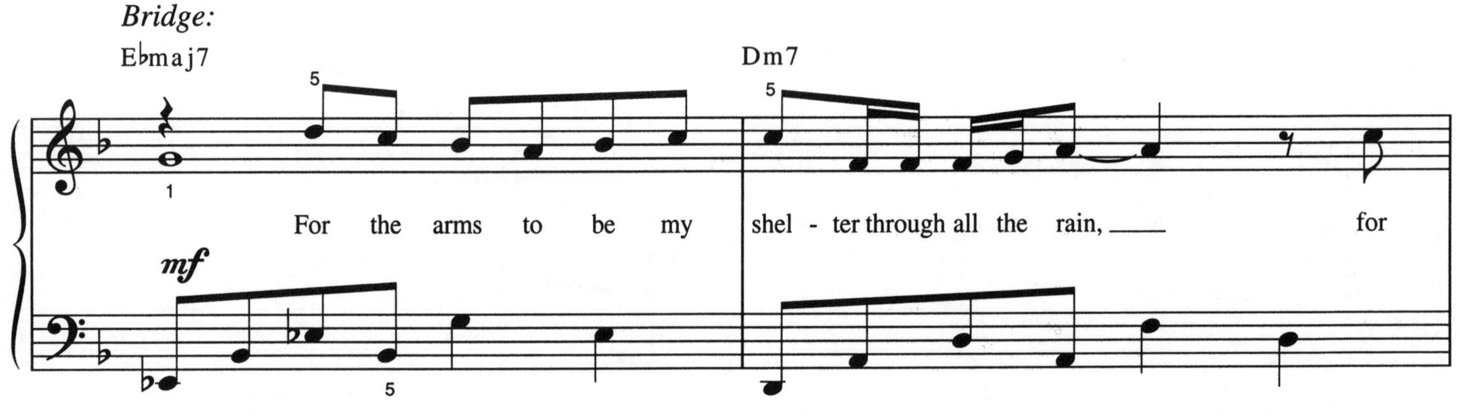
Bridge:
Ebmaj7
Dm7
For the arms to be my
shel - ter through all the rain,
for
mf

C7sus
Eb/F
F7
Eb/F
F
truth that will nev - er change,
for
some - one to lean

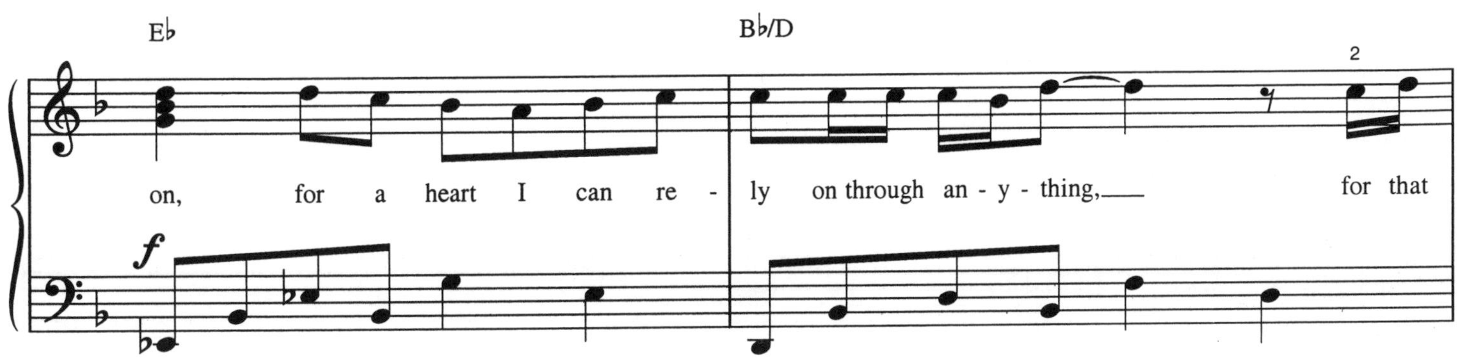
E♭
B♭/D
on, for a heart I can re - ly on through an - y - thing, for that
f

D.S. 𝄋 al Coda
Gm7/C
C7
one who I can run to. For a shield
mf

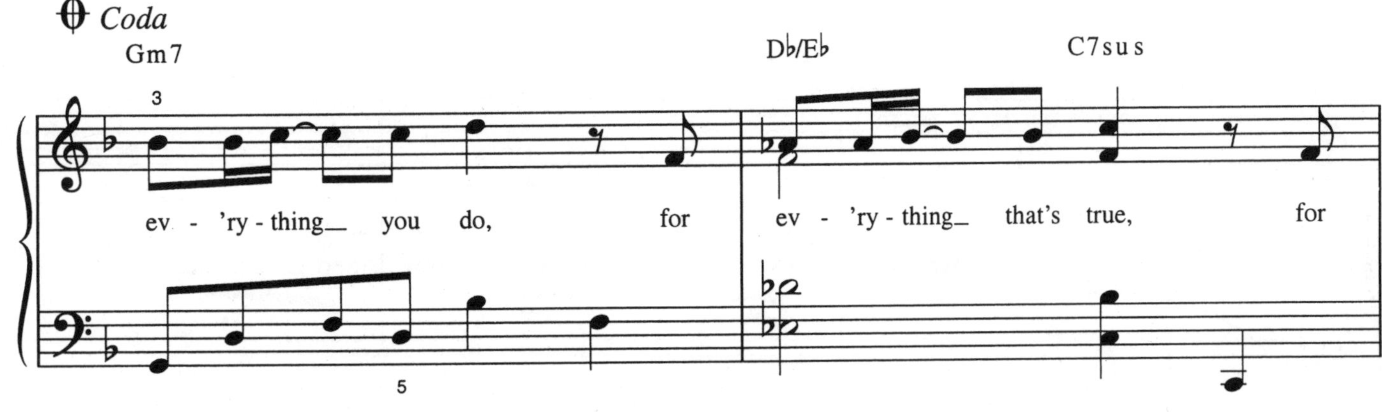
Coda
Gm7
D♭/E♭
C7sus
ev - 'ry - thing you do, for ev - 'ry - thing that's true, for

Gm7
D♭/E♭
C7sus
F
ev - 'ry - thing you do, for ev - 'ry - thing that's true, I turn to you.
molto rit.
mp

I Will Always Love You

Words and Music by Dolly Parton

F G C F/C 1. C F/G
— will al - ways love you. Bit - ter -
mp
2. D.S. al Coda
C G
I —
mp
Coda
F G
love. —
And
f
D Bm7 G A D Bm7
I — will al - ways love you. I will
Em7 A D Bm7 G A
al - ways — love you. I will al - ways — love

Extra Lyrics:

3. I hope life treats you kind
   And I hope you have all you've dreamed of.
   I wish you joy and happiness.
   But above all this,
   I wish you love.

Now And Forever

Words and Music by Richard Marx

C
B7
Em
Em/D
I lose my way, but still you seem to un - der -
I'll try to show you each and ev - 'ry way I
Un - til the day the o - cean does - n't touch the
mf
A7/C♯
Am7
G/D
D7
To Coda
stand. Now and for - ev - er, I will be your
can, now and for - ev - er, I will be your
sand, now and for - ev - er, I will be your
1.
2.
G
C/G
man.
B7
Em
C
D
Now I can rest my wor - ries and al - ways be sure
mf

Em C G D Em C
that I won't be a - lone any - more. If I'd on - ly known
G D Am7 Cm6
D.S. al Coda
you were there all the time, all the time.
Coda
G C/G Am7
man. Now and for - ev - er,
mp
C/D D C
I will be your man.
Cm G C/G D/G G
p
rit. poco a poco
pp

I'll Be There For You

Words and Music by Phil Solem, Marta Kauffman, David Crane, Michael Skloff, Allee Willis and Danny Wilde

Am
G
al - ways stuck in sec - cond gear, and it
warned you there'd be days like these. But she
F
C
Dsus4
has - n't been your day, your week, your month, or ev - en your
did - n't tell you when the world has brought you down to your
cresc. poco a poco
D
G
C
year. But
knees, that
I'll be there for you
f
D
G
when the rain starts to fall. I'll be

C
D
there for you like I've been there be-
G
C
D
fore. I'll be there for you 'cause you're
F
To Coda
1.
there for me, too.
mf
2.
G

C
3
No one could ev - er know me,
no one could ev
mf
- er see me
Em
3
since you're the
on - ly one who
knows what it's
like to be me.
Am
4
1
Some - one to face
the day with,
C/G
make it through all
the rest with,

F
C/E
D
C/E
D
some - one I'll al - ways laugh with.
Ev - en at my worst, I'm best with
Em
C
D
you.
G
C
D
D.S. al Coda
Coda
G
C
I'll be there for you

D
G
when the
rain
starts
to
fall.
I'll
be
C
D
there
for
you
like I've
been
there
be -
G
C
D
fore.
I'll
be
there
for
you
'cause you're
F
G
there
for
me,
too.
rit. e dim.
mf

Lean On Me

Words and Music by Bill Withers

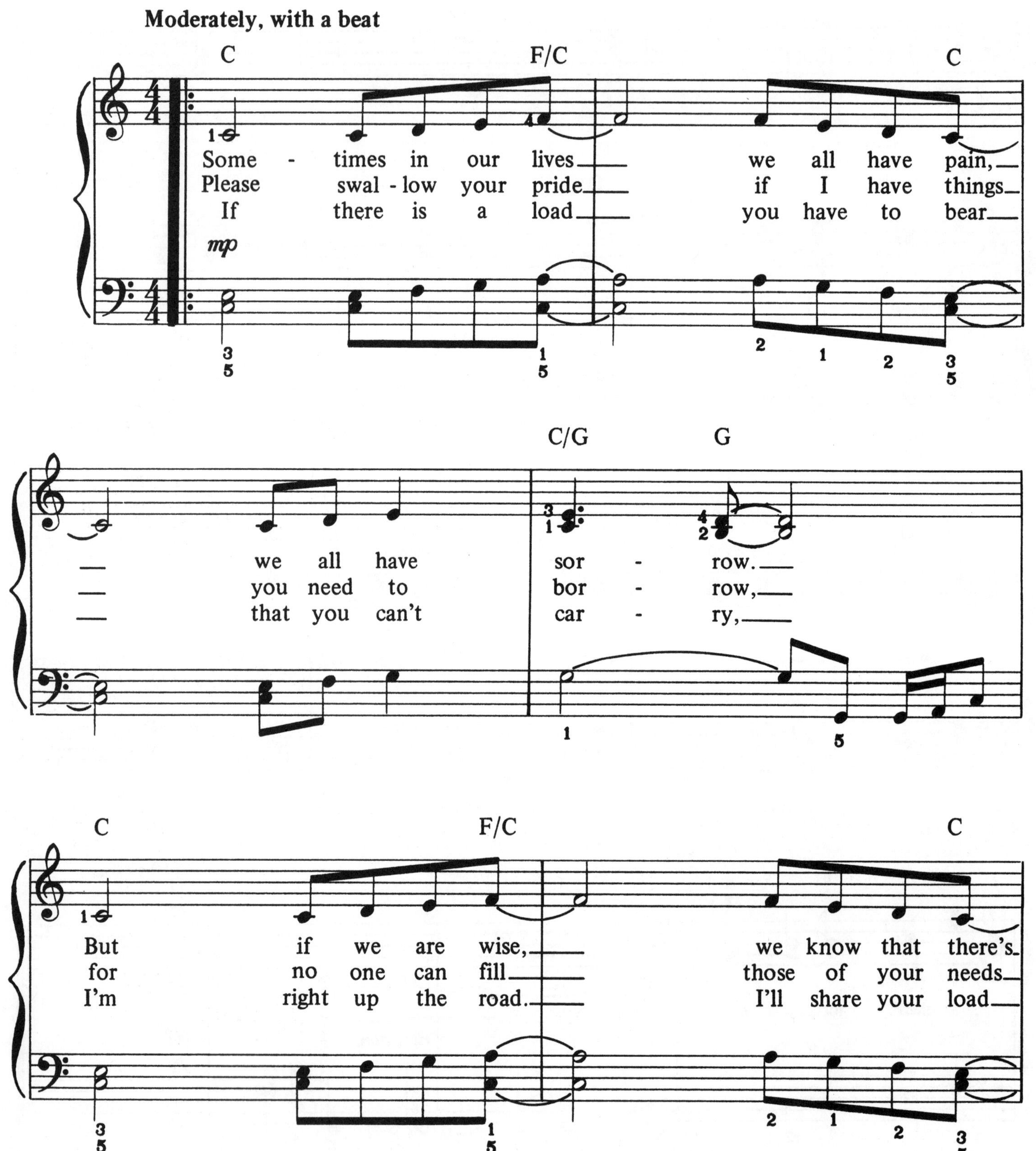

G7
C
al - ways to - mor - row.
that you won't let show.
if you just call me.
Lean on me
F
C
Em
when you're not strong and I'll be your friend. I'll help you
mf
Dm
C
F
C
car - ry on, for it won't be long till I'm gon - na need
To Coda
1.
2.
G7
C
G7
C
some-bod - y to lean on. lean on. Just

(No Chord)
call on me, broth - er, when you need a hand. We all
mp
need some-bod - y to lean on. I just might have a prob - lem that
cresc.
you'd un - der - stand. We all need some - bod - y to lean
on. Lean on me
C
F
when you're not strong
f
C
Em
Dm
and I'll be your friend. I'll help you car - ry on,

C
F
C
for it won't be long till I'm gon - na need some - bod - y to
G7
C
D.C. al Coda
lean on.
Coda
G7
C
lean on. Just
Dm/C
C
F/C
C
call me when you need a friend.
Dm/C
C
F/C
C
Call me when you need a friend.
Dm/C
C
F
C/E
Dm
C
sfz

Over The Rainbow

Words by E Y Harburg
Music by Harold Arlen

Em C7 F C/E C7
o - ver the rain - bow skies are blue,
F Fm C/G A7(♭9) D7 G7
and the dreams that you dare to dream real - ly do come
C6 C F/C G7/C
true. Some day I'll wish up - on a star and wake up where the clouds are far be -
mp
C6 G7 C
hind me, where trou - bles melt like lem - on drops, a -
mf
Edim Em7 E♭dim Dm7 G7(#5)
way a - bove the chim - ney tops that's where you'll find me.
cresc.

C Am Em C7 F C/E C7
Some - where o - ver the rain - bow blue - birds fly,
f
F Fm C/G A7(♭9) D7 G7
mf
birds fly ___ o - ver the rain - bow, why then, oh why can't
1. 2.
C6 G7 C6 C
I? I?
p
G7/C C6 G7
If
C Dm7 G7 C
mp
rit.
hap-py lit - tle blue-birds fly be - yond the rain-bow, why oh why can't I?
p
pp

The Prayer

Words and Music by Carole Bayer-Sager and David Foster

Gm
C7
Asus4
prayer
when we lose our
way.
ghie - ra
quan - ta fe - de
c'é.
mf
A
Dm
B♭
Dm
Am
Lead us to a place,
guide us with your grace
Lead us to a place,
guide us with your grace.
B♭
F/C
C7
1.
B♭
F
to a place where we'll be
safe.
2. La lu - ce che tu
Give us grace so we'll be
mp
dim.
2.
B♭/F
F
B♭
safe.
So gna - mo un
mon - do sen - za piú vio -
mf

F
B♭
F
lenza. Un mondo di giustizia e di speranza. Ognuno
B♭maj7
F
Dm
D♭
B♭m
dia la mano al suo vicino simbolo di pace, di traternità.
F7sus4
F7
3. We ask that life be
E♭
F
B♭
kind, and watch us from above.
mp

B♭/D
E♭
F
We hope each soul will find an - oth - er soul to
A♭/B♭
B♭7
Cm
love.
Let this be our prayer,
cresc.
mf
F7
D7sus4
D7
just like ev - 'ry child,
Gm
E♭
Gm
Dm
E♭
B♭/F
F7
need to find a place,
guide us with your grace.
Give us faith so we'll be
mp

Verse 2 (English lyric):
I pray we'll find your light,
And hold it in our hearts
When stars go out each night.
Let this be our prayer,
When shadows fill our day.
Lead us to a place,
Guide us with your grace.
Give us faith so we'll be safe

Verse 3 (Italian lyric):
La forza che ci dai
é il desiderio che.
Ognuno trovi amore
Intorno e dentro sé.
(Chorus:)

The Rose

Words and Music by Amanda McBroom

G
F
G
C
flow - er and
you it's on - ly
seed.
poco cresc.

C
It's the
heart a - fraid of
night has been too
mf

G
F
G
C
break - ing that
lone - ly and the
nev-er learns to
road has been too
dance. It's the
long, and you

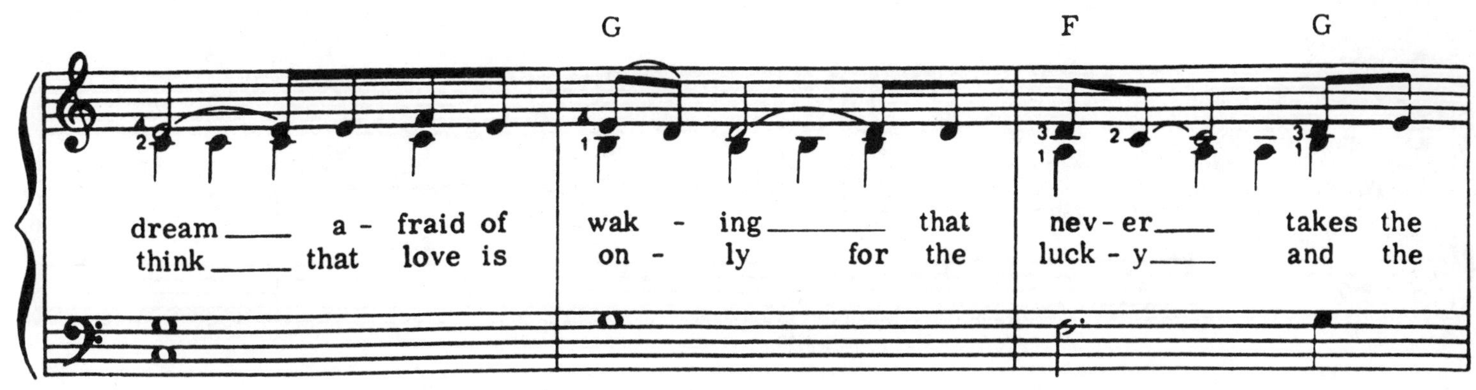
G
F
G
dream a - fraid of
think that love is
wak - ing that
on - ly for the
nev-er takes the
luck - y and the

C
Em
Am
C/G
chance. It's the one who won't be tak - en who
strong, just re - mem - ber in the win - ter far be -
F
G7
C
can not seem to give, and the soul a - fraid of
neath the bit - ter snows lies the seed that with the
1.
G
F
G
dy - ing that nev - er learns to
sun's love in the
2.
C
F
G
live.
When the spring be - comes the
cresc.
rit.
C
rose.
a tempo
rit. e dim.
p

Thank You

Words and Music by Dido Armstrong and Paul Herman

Gm
Eb
1.
Gm
Ebmaj7
wall, it re - minds me that it's not so bad, it's not so bad.
2.
Gm
Ebmaj7
not so bad, it's not so bad. And
Chorus:
Bb
I want to
mf
Eb
Bb
thank you for giv - ing me the best day of my
Eb
Bb
life. Oh, just to
Eb
Dm
Cm
Fine
be with you is hav - ing the best day of my life.

Verse 2:
I drank too much last night, got bills to pay,
My head just feels in pain.
I missed the bus and there'll be hell today,
I'm late for work again.
And even if I'm there, they'll all imply
That I might not last the day.
And then you call me and it's not so bad, it's not so bad.
(To Chorus:)

Theme from *New York, New York*

Words by Fred Ebb
Music by John Kander

F
Gm7
C7
shoes
are long- ing to
stray,
Gm
C
G7/D
C7/E
F
and step a - round the heart of it
(no lyric 2nd time)
New York, New
F7
C7/G
F7/A
B♭
York.
I wan - na
wake up in the
B♭m
F
To Coda
cit - y that does - n't
sleep
to find I'm

Am7
D7
Gm7
3
3
king of the hill,
top of the heap.
C
F
mp
My lit - tle town blues
are melt - ing a -
Gm7
C7
Gm
C
G7/D
C7/E
F
way,
I'll make a
brand new start of it
in old New
Cm7
F7
York.
mf
If I can
B♭
B♭m/D♭
F/C
D7
make it there,
I'd make it
an - y - where.

Gm7 Am7 B♭maj7 C7
It's up to you, New York, New
cresc.
F Gm7 C7
D.S. al Coda
York.
f
mf
Coda Am7 D7 Bm7
king of the hill, head of the list, cream of the crop at the
mf
D7 C/D
Slower tempo
G
top of the heap. My lit - tle town blues
rit.
f
Am7 D7 Am D A7/E D7/F♯
are melt- ing a - way, I'll make a

G
Dm7
brand new start — of it in old New York.
G7
C
Cm/E♭
mf
If I can make it there, I'd make it
G/D
E7
Am7
Bm7
an - y - where. Come on, come through New
f
Am7
C/D
G
York, New York!
ff
A♭maj7
G
sfz
8vb

There You'll Be

Words and Music by Diane Warren

C
G/B
F
look back on these days, I'll
made me make it through. I
look and see your face.
owe so much to you.

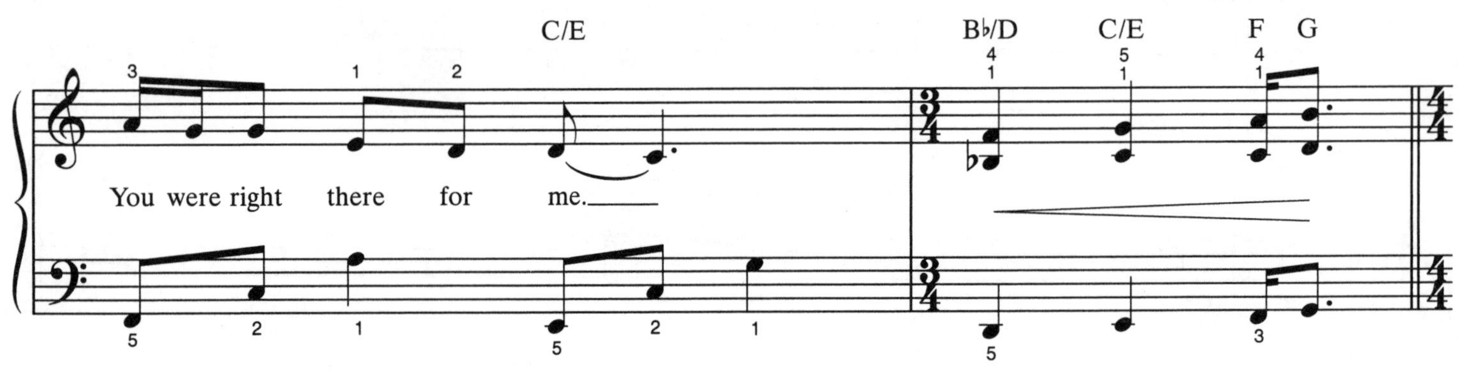
C/E
B♭/D
C/E
F G
You were right there for me.

Chorus:
Am
Em/G
F
C/E
In my dreams I'll al - ways see you soar a - bove the sky.
mf

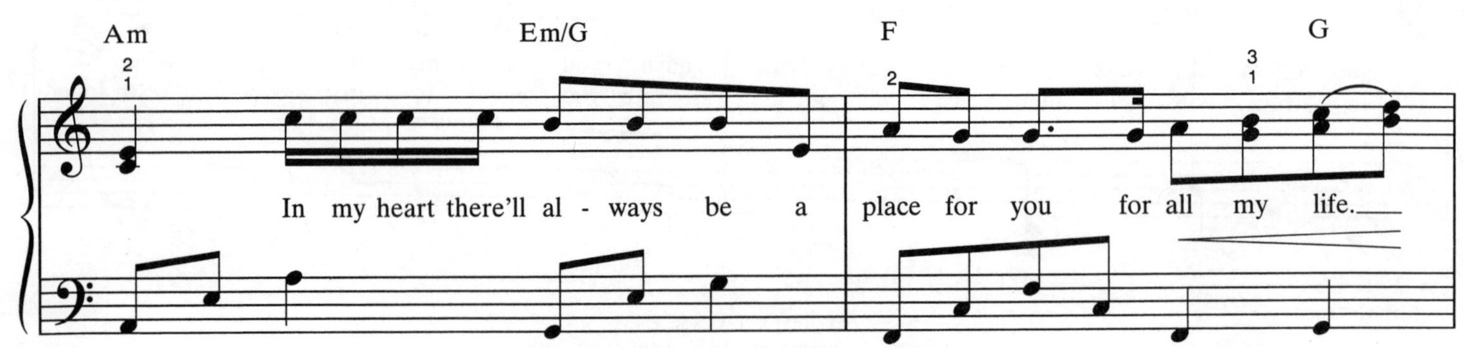
Am
Em/G
F
G
In my heart there'll al - ways be a place for you for all my life.

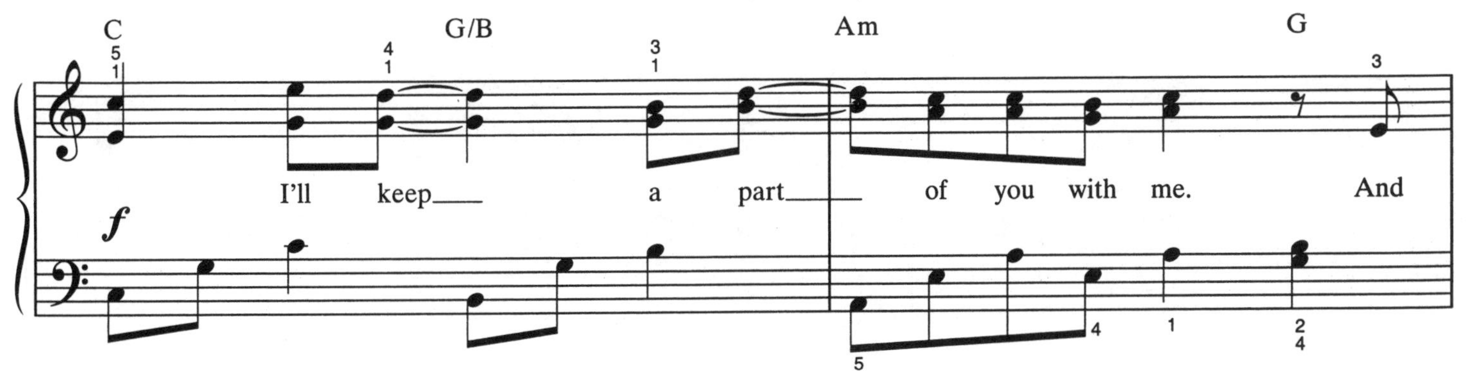
C
G/B
Am
G
I'll keep a part of you with me. And
f

1.
F
C/E
Dm7
C
ev - 'ry - where I am, there you'll be. And
mf

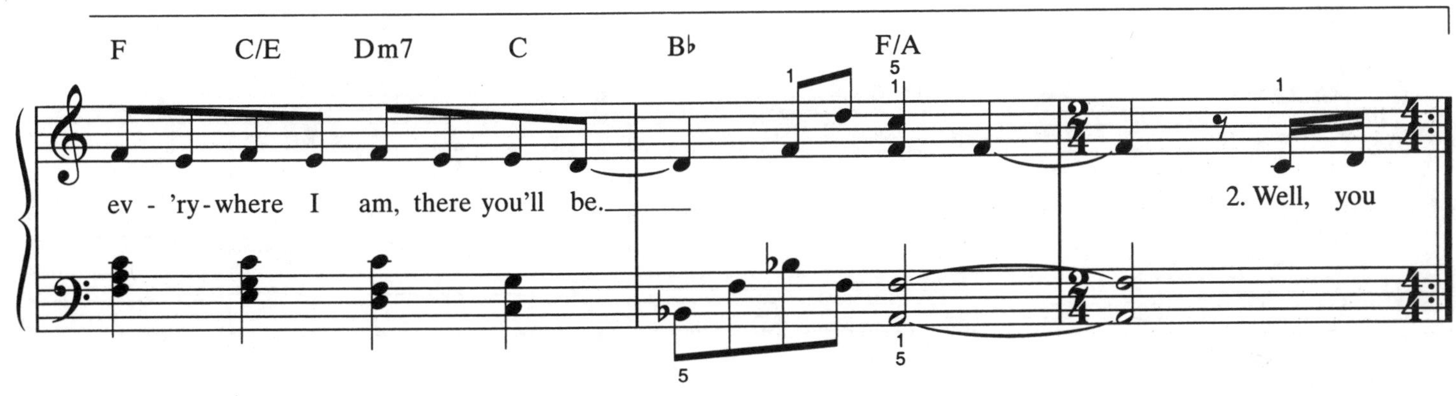
F
C/E
Dm7
C
B♭
F/A
ev - 'ry - where I am, there you'll be. 2. Well, you

2.
F
C/E
Dm7
G
C
ev - 'ry - where I am, there you'll be. 'Cause I al - ways saw in you my
mf

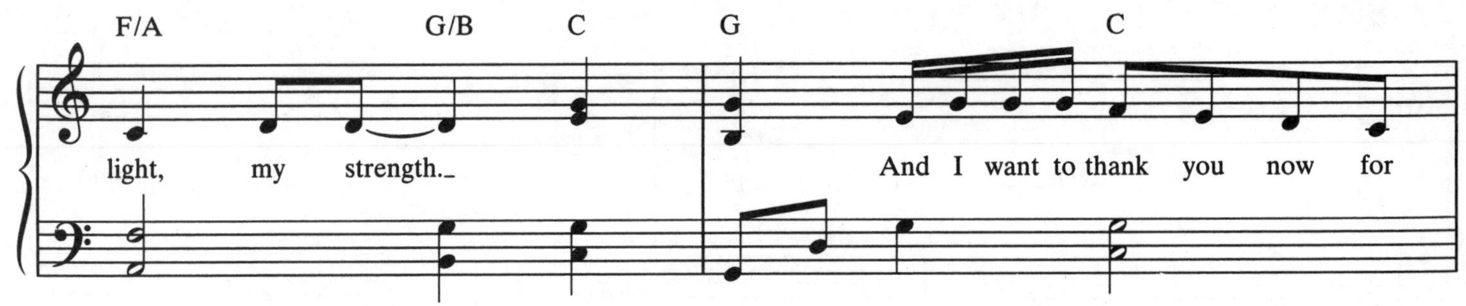
F/A
G/B
C
G
C
light, my strength._
And I want to thank you now for

Am7
F
C/E
all the ways
you were right there for me.___

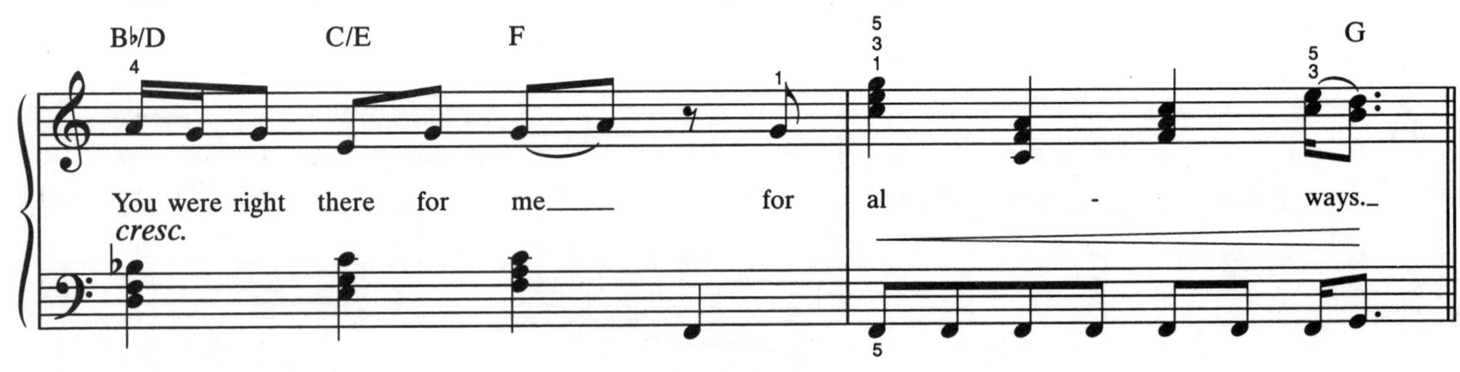
B♭/D
C/E
F
G
You were right there for me___ for al - ways._
cresc.

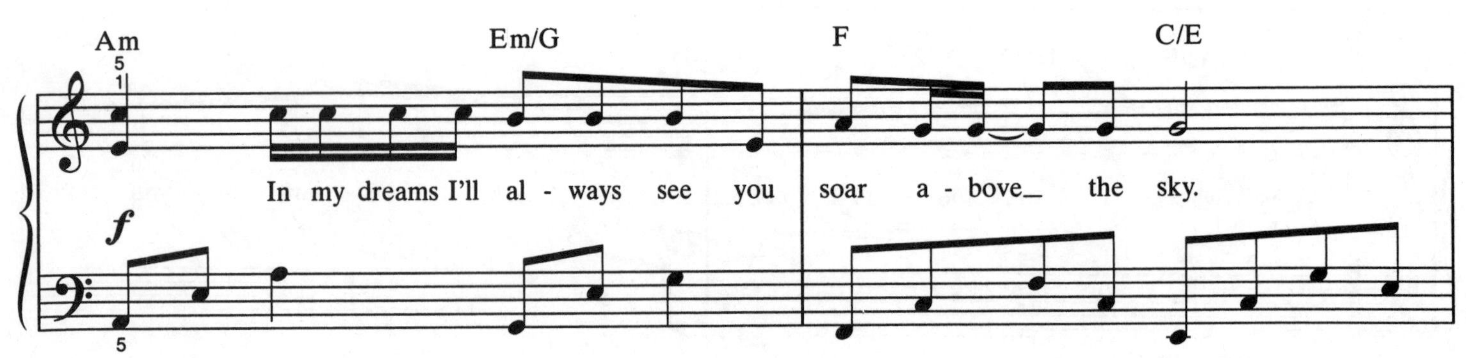
Am
Em/G
F
C/E
In my dreams I'll al - ways see you soar a - bove_ the sky.
f

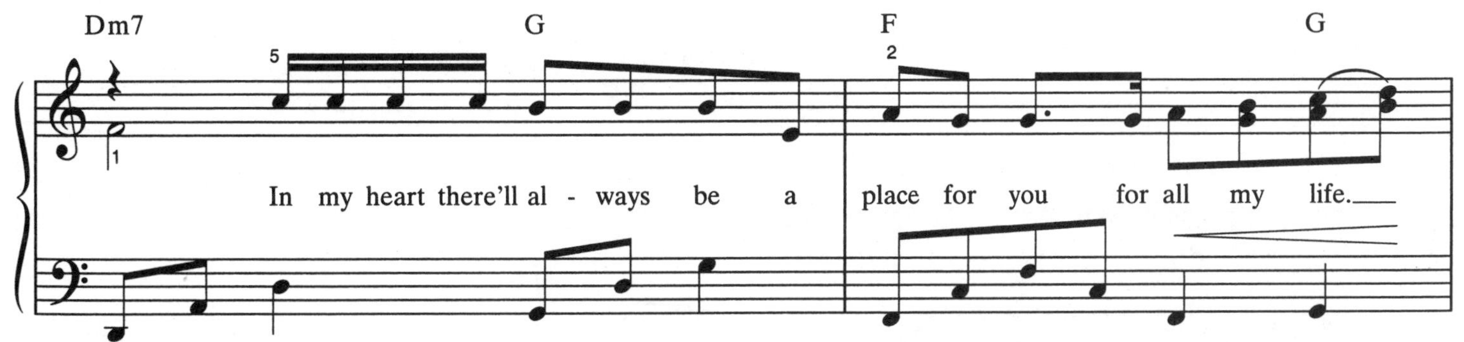
Dm7
G
F
G
In my heart there'll al - ways be a place for you for all my life.

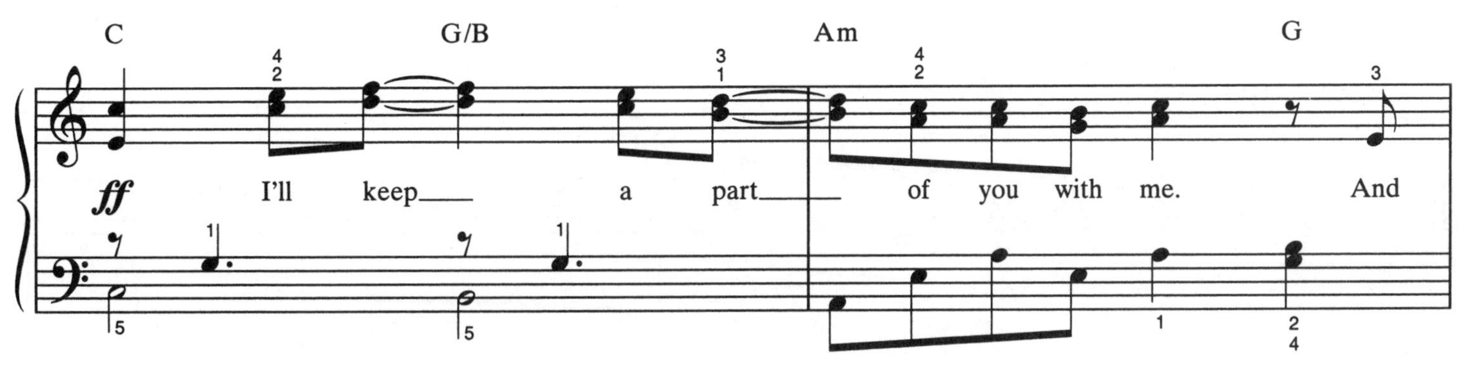
C
G/B
Am
G
ff
I'll keep a part of you with me. And

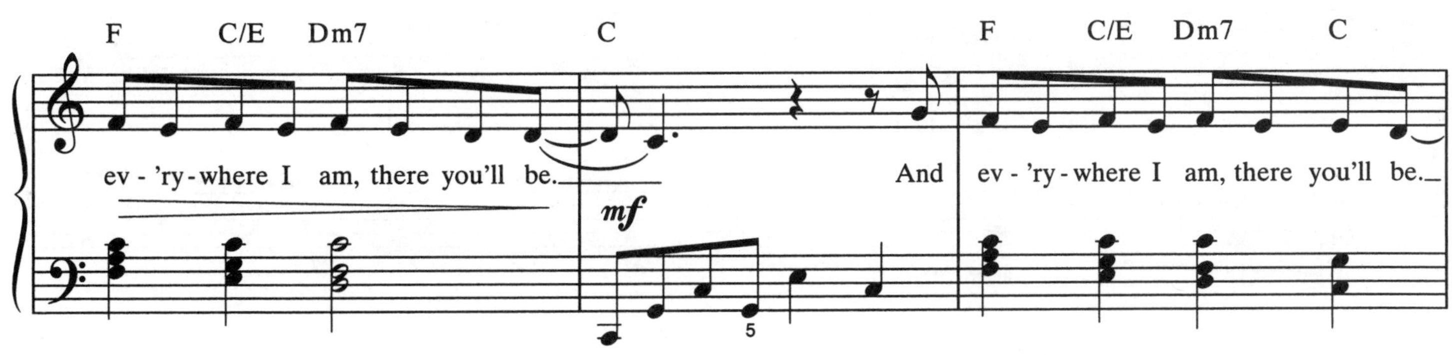
F C/E Dm7
C
F C/E Dm7 C
ev - 'ry - where I am, there you'll be.
mf
And
ev - 'ry - where I am, there you'll be.

B♭
C(9)
rit. e dim.
There you'll be.
mp

To Where You Are

Words and Music by Richard Marx and Linda Thompson

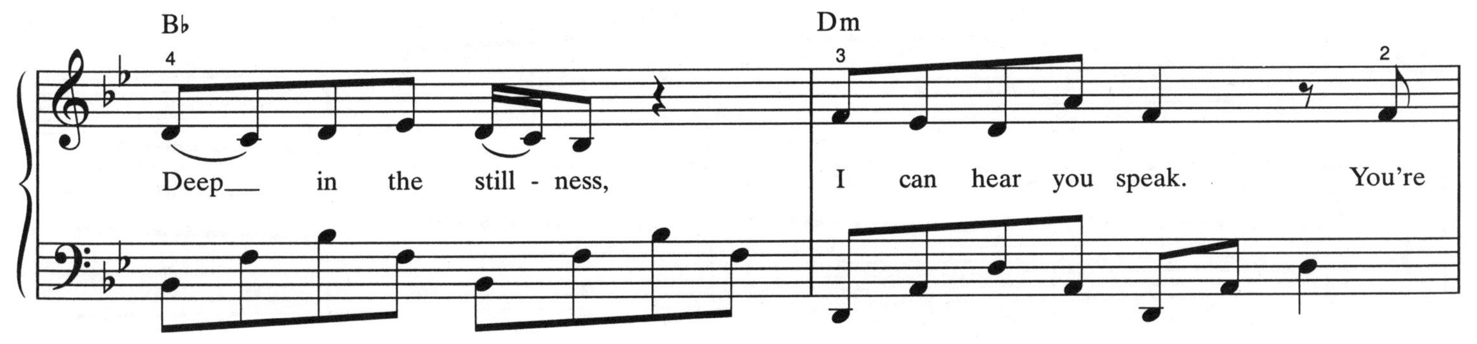
B♭
Dm
Deep__ in the still - ness,
I can hear you speak. You're

E♭m
still an in - spi - ra - tion. Can it
be___ that you are
cresc.
rit.

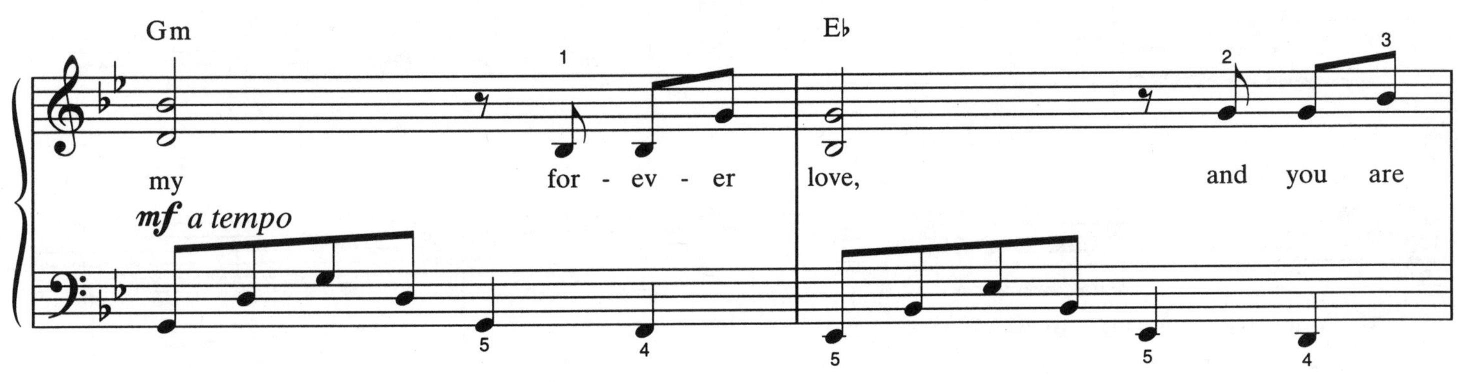
Gm
E♭
my for - ev - er
love, and you are
mf a tempo

Cm
Fsus
F
watch - ing o - ver me from up a - bove?

Chorus:
C
Dm7
C/E
F
Fly me up to where you are be - yond the dis - tant
Dm
A/C♯
F/C
G7
Em
star I wish up - on to-night to see you smile, if
Am7
Dm
on - ly for a - while to know you're there. A
Fm
To Coda
C
F/C
C
G/C
F/C
breath a - way's not far to where you are.
Verse 2:
B♭
Dm
2. Are you gen - tly sleep - ing here in - side my dream? And

E♭
B♭/F
F7
is - n't faith be - liev - ing all
pow - er can't be seen?
B♭
Dm
As my heart holds you
just one beat a - way, I
E♭m
Fsus
cher - ish all you gave me ev - 'ry
cresc.
day. 'Cause you are
Gm
E♭
my for - ev - er
mf
love watch - ing
Cm
F
me from up a -
bove. And I be -

Gm
Eb
lieve that an - gels breathe and that
Cm
Fsus
F
D.S. al Coda
love will live on and nev - er leave.
Coda
C
Am
are.
mf
I know you're
Dm
F
there. A breath a - way's not far to where you
C
G/C
F/C
C
G/C
F/C
C
are.
mp
p
rit.
r.h.

Unbreak My Heart

Words and Music by Diane Warren

A
F♯
Bm
take these tears a - way. I need your arms to
kiss this pain a - way. I can't for - get the
Em7
A
Bm
hold me now. Nights are so un - kind.
day you left. Time is so un - kind.
Bring back those nights
Life is so cruel
Em7
A
A7
when I held you be - side me.
with - out you here be - side me.
Un - break my
Dm
Gm7
C
heart, say you love me a - gain.
mf

A7
Dm
Gm7
Un - do this
hurt you caused when you
walked out the door and walked
C
A7
Dm
out of my life.
Un - cry these
tears I
Gm7
C
To Coda
A7
C/B♭
B♭
cried so man - y nights.
Un - break my
heart.
1.
A
F♯7
dim.

2.
A
F♯7
Bm
cresc.
Don't leave me in
f
Em
A
all this pain,
don't leave me out in the rain.
Bm
Em
A
A7
D.S. al Coda
Bring back those nights when I held you be - side me.
Un - break my
Coda
A7
Dm
Gm7
Un - break my,
un - break my heart, sweet ba - by.
f

C
A7
Dm
Come back and say you love me. Un - break my
Gm7
C
A7
Dm
heart, sweet dar - ling. With - out you, I just can't go on.
Gm7
C
A7
Dm
mf
Gm7
C
A7
Dm(add9)
mp rit.

The Wind Beneath My Wings

Words and Music by Larry Henley and Jeff Silbar

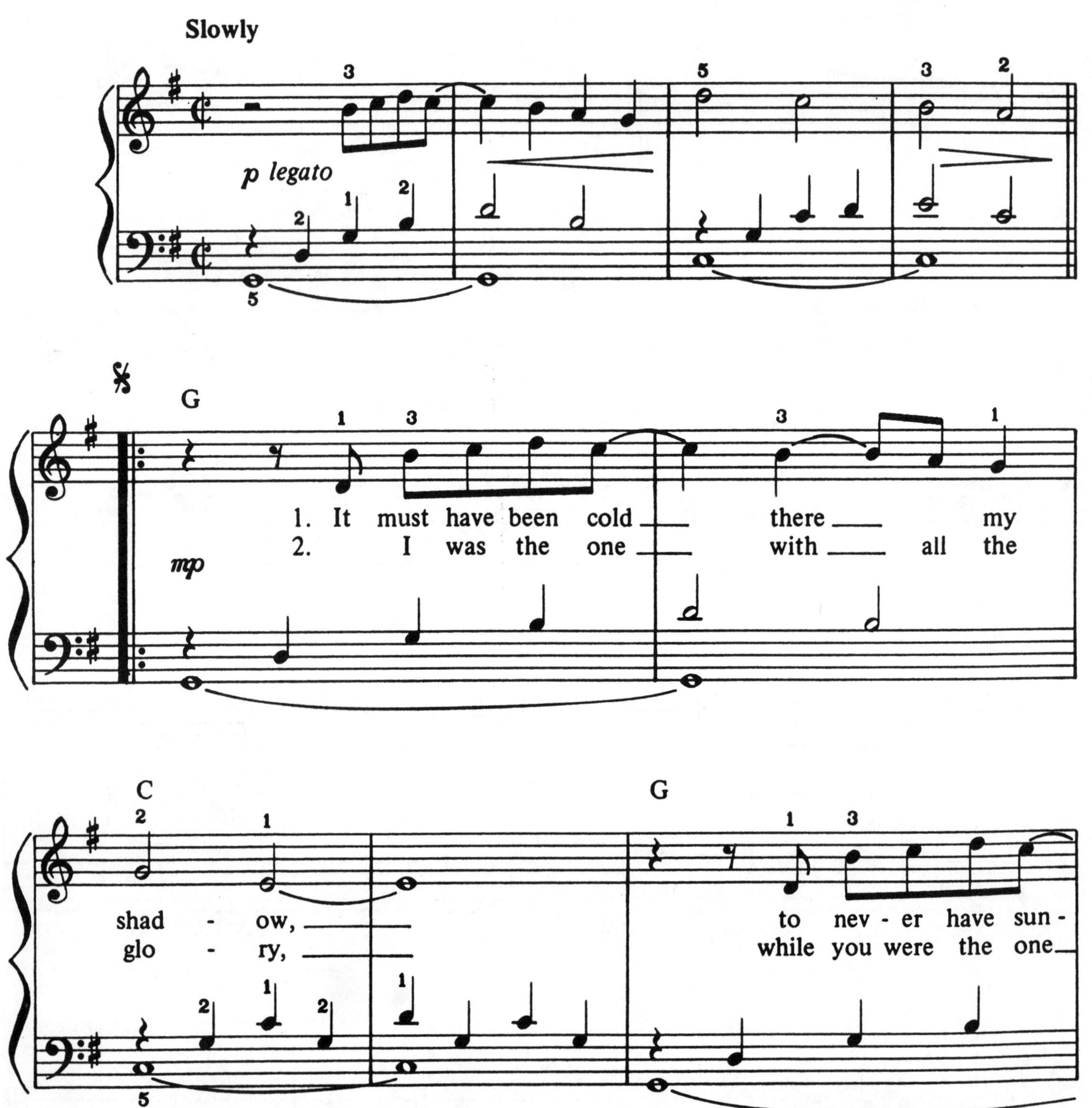

C
- light on your face.
— with all the strength,
Am
You've been con - tent to let me
on - ly a face with - out a
D7sus4
D
Am
shine,
name,
you al - ways walked
I nev - er once
1.
D7sus4
D
— the step be - hind.
— heard you com -

2.3.
D
B / D♯
Em
plain.
cresc.
mf
Did you ev - er know
C
G
that you're my
he - ro,
D / F♯
Em
and ev - 'ry - thing
C
G
I'd like to be?

D/F♯
C/E
D
Em
I can fly high-
C
Em7
E7(♭9)
- er than an
ea -
gle,
Am
Am7/D
D7
To Coda
G
'cause you are the wind __ be-neath my
wings.
D. S. 𝄋 al Coda
C

3. It might have appeared to go unnoticed
that I've got it all here in my heart.
I want you to know I know the truth:
I would be nothing without you.

You Needed Me

Words and Music by Randy Goodrum

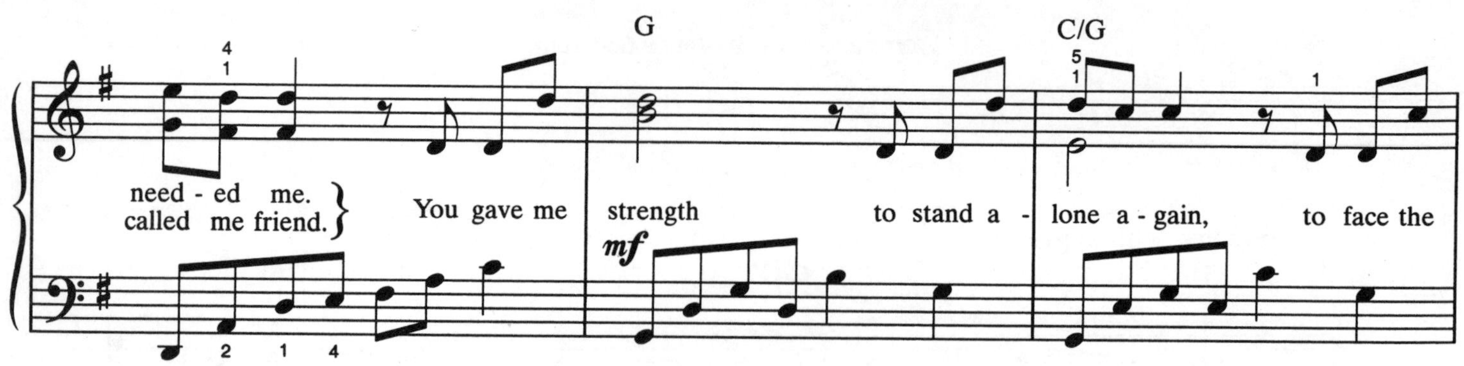
G
C/G
need - ed me.
called me friend.
You gave me
strength
to stand a -
lone a - gain,
to face the
mf

D7/G
G
Bm
world
out on my
own a - gain.
You put me
high
up - on a

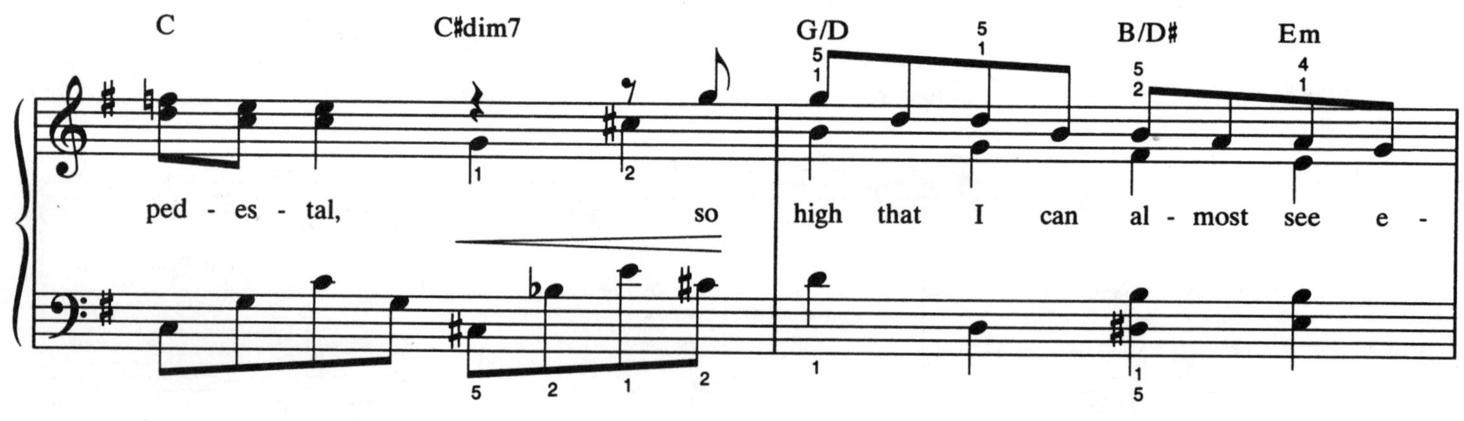
C
C♯dim7
G/D
B/D♯
Em
ped - es - tal,
so
high that I can al - most see e -

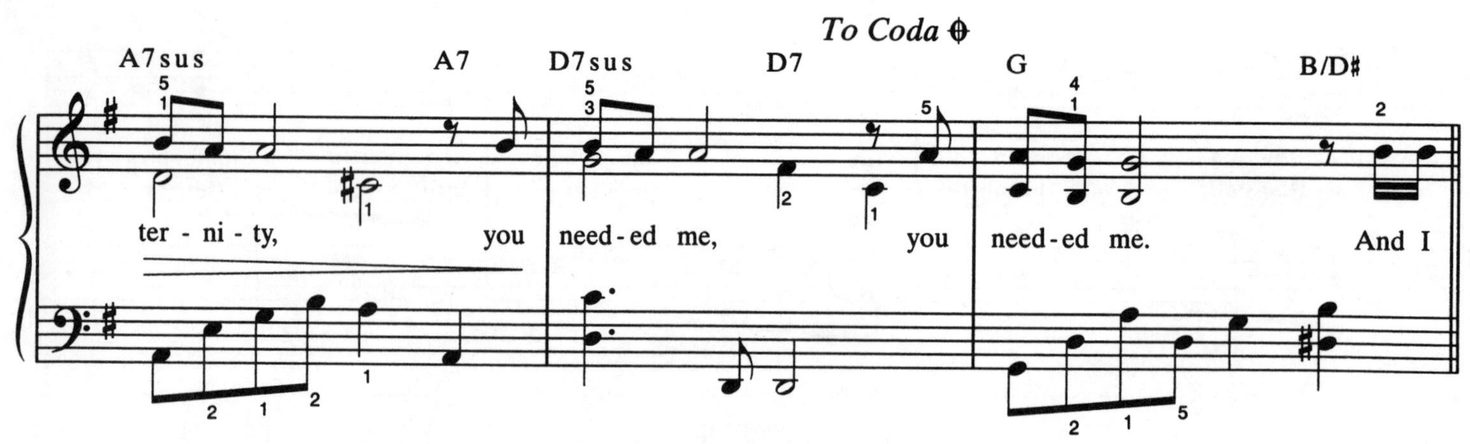
To Coda
A7sus
A7
D7sus
D7
G
B/D♯
ter - ni - ty,
you
need - ed me,
you
need - ed me.
And I

Em G/D C G/B Am7 C/D
can't be-lieve it's you, I can't be - lieve it's true. I need-ed you and you were
G B7 Em G/D
there and I'll nev - er leave. Why should I leave? I'd
C G/B A7sus A7 D7sus
be a fool 'cause I've fi-n'llyfound some-one who real-ly cares.
dim.
D.S. al Coda
C/D D7
2. You held my
Coda
G E7 A7 D7
need-ed me. You need-ed me, you
G E7 Am7 D7 G
need-ed me.
rit.

The Easy Piano Library

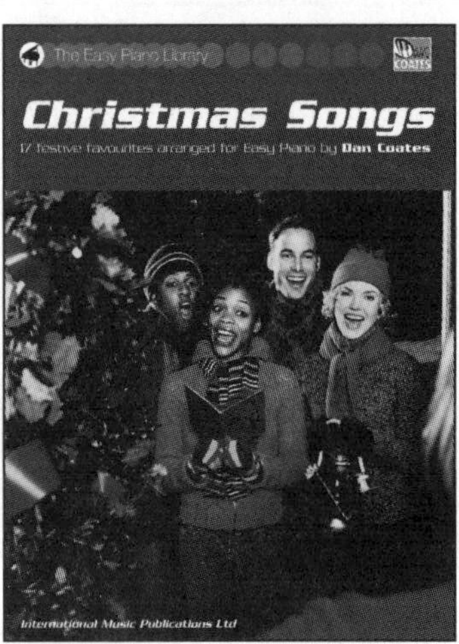

LOVE SONGS
9544A E/PNO ISBN: 1-84328-115-5

Angel Of Mine - Because You Loved Me - Get Here - The Greatest Love Of All - Have I Told You Lately That I Love You - I'd Lie For You (And That's The Truth) - I Turn To You - Now And Forever - The Prayer - Right Here Waiting - The Rose - Something About The Way You Look Tonight - Unbreak My Heart - When You Tell Me That You Love Me - 2 Become 1

POP HITS
9546A E/PNO ISBN: 1-84328-117-1

Amazed - Believe - Can't Fight The Moonlight - Genie In A Bottle - Heal The World - How Do I Live - I'll Be There For You - Kiss The Rain - Livin' La Vida Loca - Macarena - Music - Quit Playing Games With My Heart - Smooth - Swear It Again - Thank You

FILM FAVOURITES
9545A E/PNO ISBN: 1-84328-116-3

Batman Theme - Beautiful Stranger - Because You Loved Me - Can You Feel The Love Tonight - Can't Fight The Moonlight - Evergreen - (Everything I Do) I Do It For You - I Don't Want To Miss A Thing - Imperial March (Darth Vader's Theme) - I Will Always Love You - Somewhere My Love (Lara's Theme) - Star Wars (Main Theme) - Superman Theme - Wind Beneath My Wings

ALL TIME GREATS
9603A E/PNO ISBN: 1-84328-138-4

American Pie – As Time Goes By – Desperado – The Greatest Love Of All – Hotel California – Lean On Me – My Heart Will Go On – My Way – Over The Rainbow – Sacrifice – Save The Best For Last – Send In The Clowns – Stairway To Heaven – Theme From New York, New York – When You Tell Me That You Love Me

GREAT SONGWRITERS
9671A E/PNO ISBN: 1-84328-175-3

As Time Goes By – Bewitched – Cabaret – High Hopes – I Got Plenty O' Nuttin' – It Ain't Necessarily So – Love & Marriage – Maybe This Time – Never Met A Man I Din't Like – Over The Rainbow – Raindrops Keep Fallin' On My Head – Send In The Clowns – Singin' In The Rain – Summertime – Tomorrow

CHRISTMAS SONGS
9790A E/PNO ISBN: 1-84328-309-3

All I Want For Christmas Is My Two Front Teeth - Deck The Hall - It's The Most Wonderful Time Of The Year - Jingle Bells - Let it Snow! Let it Snow! Let it Snow! - The Little Drummer Boy - Little Saint Nick - Have Yourself A Merry Little Christmas - I Believe In Santa Claus - The Most Wonderful Day Of The Year - O Christmas Tree - Rockin' Around The Christmas Tree - Rudolph, The Red-Nosed Reindeer - Santa Claus Is Comin' To Town - Sleigh Ride - The Twelve Days Of Christmas - Winter Wonderland

An expansive series of over 50 titles!

Each song features melody line, vocals, chord displays, suggested registrations and rhythm settings.

"For each title ALL the chords (both 3 finger and 4 finger) used are shown in the correct position - which makes a change!" **Organ & Keyboard Cavalcade, May 2001**

Each song appears on two facing pages eliminating the need to turn the page during performance. We have just introduced a new cover look to the series and will repackage the backlist in the same way.

Big Band Hits .19098
Blues .3477A
Broadway .9888A
Celebration Songs .3478A
Christmas Carols .4616A
Christmas Songs .19198
Classic Hits Volume 1 .19099
Classic Hits Volume 2 .19100
Cliff Richard .9030A
Cole Porter .10041A
Country Songs .19101
Disco .9394A
Eighties, The .2975A
Elton John .5779A
English Favourites .4229A
Favourite Hymns .4179A
Fifties, The .2972A
Film Classics .19197
Forties, The .2971A
Frank Sinatra .9025A
George & Ira Gershwin .9804A
George Michael .7646A
Gilbert & Sullivan .9707A
Glenn Miller .5772A
Great Songwriters .2225A
I Try Plus 10 More Chart Hits .5778A
Instrumental Classics .2338A
James Bond .9236A
Jazz Classics .5770A
Latin Collection .5777A
Love Songs Volume 1 .19102
Love Songs Volume 2 .19199
Motown Classics .2337A
Music Hall .3329A
Nineties, The .2976A
Number One Hits .19200
Number One Hits Volume 2 .9787A
Popular Classics .4180A
Pub Singalong Collection .3954A
Queen .9714A
Robbie Williams Easy Keyboard .9501A
Rock 'n' Roll Classics .2224A
Scott Joplin .9738A
Seventies, The .2974A
Shirley Bassey .9350A
Showtunes Volume 1 .19103
Showtunes Volume 2 .3328A
Sixties, The .2973A
Soft Rock Collection .4617A
Soul Classics .19201
Thirties, The .2970A
Traditional English Favourites .4229A
Traditional Irish Favourites .4230A
Traditional Scottish Favourites .4231A
TV Themes .19196
Twenties, The .2969A
Wartime Collection .3955A
Wedding Collection .3688A
Whitney Houston .7647A

YOU'RE THE VOICE

8861A PV/CD

Casta Diva from Norma – Vissi D'arte from Tosca – Un Bel Di Vedremo from Madama Butterfly – Addio, Del Passato from La Traviata – J'ai Perdu Mon Eurydice from Orphee Et Eurydice – Les Tringles Des Sistres Tintaient from Carmen – Porgi Amor from Le Nozze Di Figaro – Ave Maria from Otello

8860A PVG/CD

Delilah – Green Green Grass Of Home – Help Yourself – I'll Never Fall In Love Again – It's Not Unusual – Mama Told Me Not To Come – Sexbomb – Thunderball – What's New Pussycat – You Can Leave Your Hat On

9297A PVG/CD

Beauty And The Beast – Because You Loved Me – Falling Into You – The First Time Ever I Saw Your Face – It's All Coming Back To Me Now – Misled – My Heart Will Go On – The Power Of Love – Think Twice – When I Fall In Love

9349A PVG/CD

Chain Of Fools – A Deeper Love Do Right Woman, Do Right Man – I Knew You Were Waiting (For Me) – I Never Loved A Man (The Way I Loved You) – I Say A Little Prayer – Respect – Think – Who's Zooming Who – (You Make Me Feel Like) A Natural Woman

9007A PVG/CD

Careless Whisper – A Different Corner – Faith – Father Figure – Freedom '90 – I'm Your Man – I Knew You Were Waiting (For Me) – Jesus To A Child – Older – Outside

9606A PVG/CD

Don't Let Me Be Misunderstood – Feeling Good – I Loves You Porgy – I Put A Spell On You – Love Me Or Leave Me – Mood Indigo – My Baby Just Cares For Me – Ne Me Quitte Pas (If You Go Away) – Nobody Knows You When You're Down And Out – Take Me To The Water

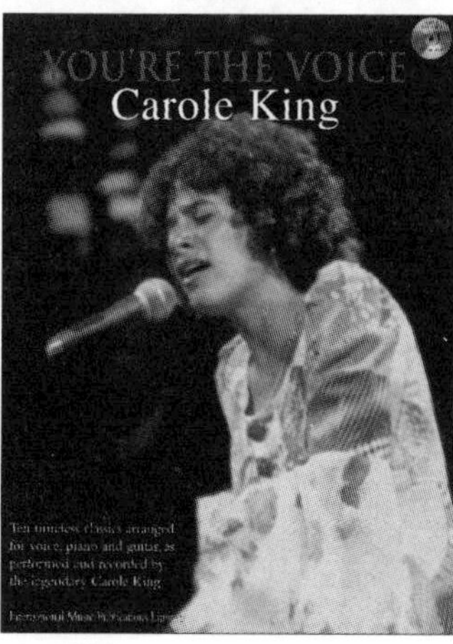

9700A PVG/CD

Beautiful – Crying In The Rain – I Feel The Earth Move – It's Too Late – (You Make Me Feel Like) A Natural Woman – So Far Away – Way Over Yonder – Where You Lead – Will You Love Me Tomorrow – You've Got A Friend

9746A PVG/CD

April In Paris – Come Rain Or Come Shine – Fly Me To The Moon (In Other Words) – I've Got You Under My Skin – The Lady Is A Tramp – My Kinda Town (Chicago Is) – My Way – Theme From *New York, New York* – Someone To Watch Over Me – Something Stupid

9770A PVG/CD

Cry Me A River – Evergreen (A Star Is Born) – Happy Days Are Here Again – I've Dreamed Of You – Memory – My Heart Belongs To Me – On A Clear Day (You Can See Forever) – Someday My Prince Will Come – Tell Him (duet with Celine Dion) – The Way We Were

9799A PVG/CD

Boogie Woogie Bugle Boy – Chapel Of Love – Friends – From A Distance – Hello In There – One For My Baby (And One More For The Road) – Only In Miami – The Rose – When A Man Loves A Woman – Wind Beneath My Wings

9810A PVG/CD

Ain't No Sunshine – Autumn Leaves – How Can I Keep From Singing – Imagine – It Doesn't Matter Anymore – Over The Rainbow – Penny To My Name – People Get Ready – Wayfaring Stranger – What A Wonderful World

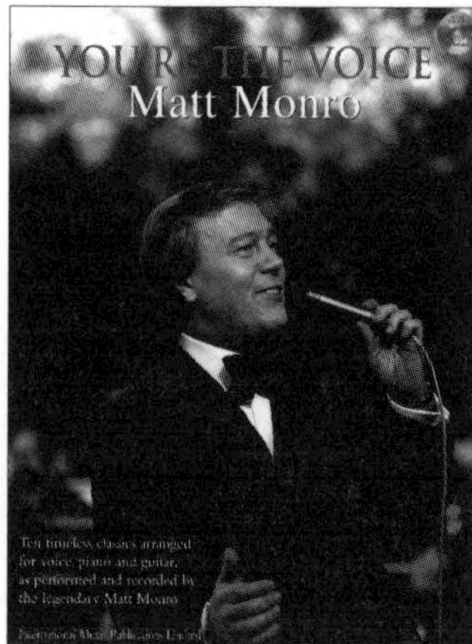

9889A PVG/CD

Around The World – Born Free – From Russia With Love – Gonna Build A Mountain – The Impossible Dream – My Kind Of Girl – On A Clear Day You Can See Forever – Portrait Of My Love – Softly As I Leave You – Walk Away

The outstanding vocal series from IMP

CD contains full backings for each song, professionally arranged to recreate the sounds of the original recording